Endorsements

This book isn't only for widows. It's also for those who love them. *Widow's Might* invites those of us on the sidelines of a tragic loss—who are uncertain of how to help—to better understand the confusing, unpredictable road of grief as well as the challenges and promise of new growth. Kim Knight's words will break your heart, make you think, and help you stand steadfastly beside those facing the death of a spouse. Buy a copy for yourself and one for anyone you know who's lost the love of their life.

—Vicki Kuyper, author of *A Tale of Two Biddies*
and *Wonderlust*

I spent thirty-five years on Wall Street and during that time I never met a person quite like Dale, who had the perfect balance between business life and family life. Much of that balance was because of his truly special relationship with his wife, Kim. After Dale died, I sent Kim a note which read, *I can count on one hand—no, make that one finger—the number of wholesalers' wives who were a bigger part of their spouse's business than you were with Dale.* *Widow's Might* is the story of how one widow moved forward to embrace life's challenges, to find joy in devastating circumstances, and to encourage others sharing the journey to get back in the game.

—Dr. Bob Froehlich, former vice chairman
of Deutsche Asset Management

I can't think of anyone better to write a book on how to navigate such a complex topic that none of us is particularly well equipped to handle. Nevertheless, in *Widow's Might* Kim shares the unexpected journey she had to navigate as a reflection of the kind of person she is—and we can all aspire to be. She shows the very human struggles associated with losing your partner, your friend, and your love. She asks the difficult questions that any person would have but may not readily admit. Yet, she also follows those questions with a determination to use this very painful chapter in her life as another means to show how her faith in Christ enables her to be a beacon for those around her.

—Doug Davis, senior vice president, industry-leading
Fortune 100 company

As a seasoned financial advisor, I've been blessed with the privilege of assisting a number of clients as they've traveled the uncharted and difficult journey which Kim so transparently and openly shares in her amazing book. Kim answers the two basic questions that I've been asked repeatedly through the years: 1) "Is this how I am supposed to feel?" and 2) "What did your other clients do when this happened to them?" Every person takes a little different route as they navigate the emotional, physical, psychological, spiritual, and financial challenges that come all bundled up in the overwhelming event of losing a husband/friend/spiritual partner. Kim shares in a powerful and effective way how she has grieved, cried, grown, and even learned to celebrate life again on this road that no one ever wants to travel. *Widow's Might* is an incredible guide for anyone who has lost their spouse, and it's also an excellent resource for those of us who are the friends, family members, and professional advisors to those who have experienced this type of life-changing loss.

—Lance D. Marble, president, Wealth Professionals, LLC

As a pastor I am always looking for practical resources for ministry opportunities. I was hoping that this might be one, but I was worried that it would be more of a processing tool for Kim to work through her grave loss. So, I was very pleased to see that this is not only a riveting account of her journey through this sudden loss but also an extremely relevant and practical book. The way Kim describes her journey and the way she connects it to practical "takeaways" and lessons is spectacular. *Widow's Might* will be a for-sure resource as a pastor, and I will recommend it for all those who are forced to grieve the loss of a dear spouse. Thank you, Kim!

—Kevin Wood, lead pastor,
First Baptist Church of Ukiah, CA

I was honored to be in the room with the family when they said their final good-byes to their father, brother, and loving husband. Throughout the shocking and heartbreaking process, it was remarkable how emotionally aware and spiritually strong Kim was. It came as no surprise to me that she felt nudged to write about her experience. *Widow's Might* offers honest and thoughtful guidance to others who have experienced loss.

—Allan Fuller, senior pastor,
Mountain Park Community Church, AZ

In my thirty-four years as a wealth manager, I've helped many women who have survived the loss of a spouse or partner. Together we work through the turmoil to make the best financial decisions at one of the most difficult times of their lives. Grief, fear, and uncertainty make choices incredibly challenging. Yet finances are only one aspect of their lives that have completely changed, and Kim's book is a terrific resource. Her words are filled with the warmth of a comforting friend and can help anyone navigate the new and disorienting circumstances of widowhood. I highly recommend *Widow's Might* to anyone who has lost a spouse.

—Deborah L. Danielson, CFP®, CFS®, MSFS, president and owner of Danielson Financial Group; investment professional since 1981 with a master of science in financial services; CERTIFIED FINANCIAL PLANNER™ and Certified Fund Specialist

Widow's Might

Embracing Life after the Loss of Your Spouse

Kim Knight

BroadStreet
PUBLISHING

BroadStreet Publishing Group, LLC
Racine, Wisconsin, USA
BroadStreetPublishing.com

Widow's Might: Embracing Life after the Loss of Your Spouse

Copyright © 2016 by Karen Kim Knight

ISBN-13: 978-1-4245-5111-8 (softcover)
ISBN-13: 978-1-4245-5112-5 (e-book)

Stock or custom editions of BroadStreet Publishing titles may be purchased in bulk for educational, business, ministry, fundraising, or sales promotional use. For information, please e-mail info@ broadstreetpublishing.com.

Cover design by Chris Garborg, garborgdesign.com
Interior design and typeset by Katherine Lloyd, TheDESKonline.com

Printed in the United States of America

16 17 18 19 20 5 4 3 2 1

Dedicated with admiration to those who
have traveled this road and prevailed,

With gratitude to the friends who journeyed with us,

And with love to my mother, Jo Koeneman,
who held my hand along the way.

May God hold you in the palm of His hand.

Contents

1. Life Changes in an Instant 11

2. What's the Password? 23

3. Life Changes . . . Over Time 39

4. When the Casserole Days Are Over 45

5. What's in His Pockets? 55

6. Where Was God When I Needed Him? 63

7. Is My Spouse in Heaven? 75

8. Who Am I Now? 83

9. Does Life Continue in Your Husband's Home? 93

10. Dating after Twenty-Five Years
    of Marriage . . . or Fifty 103

11. Oh My Goodness! I Met Someone New 111

12. Dealing with the Guilt of Surviving...and
    Being Happy Again 121

13. What Do I Want to Be When I Grow Up? 133

14. Life Is Short—Get Back in the Game 141

Notes 151
Acknowledgments 155
About the Author 157

1

Life Changes in an Instant

The phone call came at 9:30 a.m. on Monday, March 4, 2013.

"Mrs. Knight. This is Justin from Chase Bank. Mr. Knight is here and he's had some kind of . . . seizure. And the paramedic wants to talk to you."

Seizure? What kind of seizure? Dale had left the house fifteen minutes earlier to open a checking account for the franchise we'd just purchased on Friday. He was dressed in his usual navy blazer and slacks, and I'd asked where he was going.

"To the bank to open a corporate checking account."

"What name are you thinking?"

"I'm thinking Dale Knight Enterprises."

"What about Kim Knight Enterprises?"

We'd laughed and away he went. Now I was telling a paramedic what kind of medication he took and that, yes, he did have high blood pressure.

When I asked where they were taking Dale, the paramedic named a nearby hospital.

"Oh, couldn't you please take him to Banner Desert?" It was the hospital my neighbor had told me was the best when I first moved to town.

The short answer was, "No. We go to the nearest hospital."

I'd been working on my taxes at the kitchen table and was still in my pajamas. I ran to get dressed, jumped in my car, and sped to the hospital. My mind was racing. What kind of seizure? Is he conscious? How do I get to the hospital? Where do I park?

The receptionist in the emergency room sent me to a small cubicle. Dale was in a hospital gown, and the ER doc was examining him. It appeared Dale had suffered a stroke—his speech was impaired, he couldn't move his left side—all the "traditional" stroke symptoms.

Dale motioned me to come closer and I leaned down. "What do you need, honey?"

"They wadded up my blazer and put it in that plastic bag over there. I want you to hang it up!"

I laughed out loud! So Dale. He's in the ER having a stroke, and he wants me to hang up his blazer! I dug it out of the bag and hung it up. I learned in that moment the lesson of taking my joy where I could find it. There wouldn't be many opportunities that day—or in the foreseeable future.

The ER doc explained that he thought Dale had suffered a stroke, and he wanted to know if I would give my permission for them to give Dale an antistroke medication called a TPA (tissue plasminogen activator). He had a chart that explained when the TPA was given to stroke victims within two hours of the onset of the stroke, about 20 percent greatly improved, 80 percent remained the same, and 3 percent died. Died! Did

Dale have any type of bleeding disorder? If he did, this would kill him.

"No bleeding disorder," I told the doctor. "What would *you* do?"

I can't remember what he said, but I thought, *I have to call my mom.* My dad had died of an intracranial hemorrhage a year and a half earlier. Mom would know what to do.

"Mom." I started crying. "Mom, Dale's had some type of stroke. I'm in the emergency room and the doctor wants to know if I'll agree to let him administer this stroke medicine to Dale." I did my best to explain what the doc had said, and we decided to go ahead with the TPA.

Mom said, "I'm getting on a plane as soon as I can. I'll be there tomorrow."

I hung up and called my church, Mountain Park Community Church. They were the only people I could think of who would be "home." My friend Cindy is the receptionist. When she answered the phone, I explained my situation and asked her to please send someone to the ER.

Allan, our senior pastor, was in a meeting all day, but she would send Greg, another pastor.

The ER doc handed me a stack of papers to sign indicating I knew the risks involved in administering the TPA, and he prepped Dale to receive the drug. The doctor lowered the head of Dale's bed, and instantly Dale was better! His speech was perfect; he could move his left side.

I looked at the doctor. "Oh my God! He's going to be all right!"

The doctor looked stricken. "No, Kim. That means something else is wrong. Dale didn't magically get better."

They took Dale away for an ultrasound to try to determine what was happening.

I had a minute to catch my breath and to figure out what I should do. A woman from the hospital arrived to ask me to fill out admission papers. Do we have insurance? Where's my insurance card? Please fill out this medical history. Do you have a religious preference? Can we send someone down to be with you?

I completed the paperwork. Another woman from the hospital chapel came to pray with me. I kept thinking, *Is this a Christian hospital? Do they know I'm a Christian?* It's not. They didn't.

The women left and I called a few friends. No one was home.

They brought Dale back and moved us to another cubicle. This one was bigger and directly across from the ER nurses' station. I brought Dale's blazer (hanging up) and the rest of his stuff—still jammed in the bag.

Dale hadn't had a stroke. He'd suffered an aneurysm of his aorta—something I later learned is called an aortic dissection. His aorta had split on the inside, right at the top of the aortic arch, which is directly above the heart.

Dale was talking and full of questions and information. "Do they think I had a stroke?"

"They did. But you really had an aneurysm in your aorta."

"When I was at the bank, I had a terrible pain in my neck."

Dale's stepmother, a cardiovascular surgical nurse, told me later that perhaps his carotid artery had collapsed—cutting off the oxygen supply to Dale's brain, mimicking the stroke symptoms.

Dale then turned to the ER doc. "I think I should tell you that I have a terrible pain in my thigh."

The ER doc and the nurse exchanged a glance that said, *Oh, this is not good.*

I asked the nurse, "What does that mean?"

She said the fact that his thigh was in such pain meant his aorta had dissected all the way down to his thigh.

"How do you fix that?"

"Where is your family?" she asked.

"California."

"You should call them right now."

"Will they get here in time?"

"Probably not." Probably not? It's only a six-hour drive.

I called my son, Beau. Dale was Beau's stepdad, and they'd always had a close relationship. Beau said he would call his sister, Erin, and bring her and his wife, Meagan, to Phoenix as soon as he could.

I called Dale's brother, Cole, who lives in San Diego. He had jury duty the next day but said he would tell them he couldn't stay, and then he'd drive to Phoenix as soon as possible. Dale's sister, Dana, was getting ready for a job interview in Texas, so I left her a message to call me when she could. Dale's mom was in the hospital in Little Rock, Arkansas. I called her husband to tell him the news.

"That doesn't sound good," he said.

"It's not good, Jim. I'll call you when I can."

I returned to Dale's "room," and the ER doc was frantically calling every cardiovascular surgeon in the area. No one was available. At one point, he thought someone might be available in Flagstaff, Arizona. When I told Dale they might fly him there to do surgery, he said, "Well, get my clothes and I'll get dressed!"

Oh my gosh! Only Dale would want to look "snappy" on his Flight for Life to Flagstaff! Before the decision was confirmed, however, the doctor in Flagstaff got another patient. Option closed.

Pastor Greg showed up with Gene, a longtime friend from our small group Bible study. Dale was excited to see them! Honestly, for all of our married life, Dale was not an ideal patient. Truth be told, I'm not a great nurse, either. It was really unbelievable that Dale was in such great spirits, given the circumstances. It was truly a gift from God that he seemed to be unaware of how grave his situation was.

Word started to get out that Dale was in the hospital, and friends and neighbors began to arrive. With each new friend, Dale would say, "Is that so-and-so? I can't believe you're here! How are you?" Greg and Dale talked golf and sports cars. Friends said prayers. People visited with each other. Everyone except Dale knew he was in trouble, but it was almost a festive scene.

The ER doc was still calling surgeons when I heard him say, "I don't care. I *need* you to come. There isn't anyone else, and you're only a mile away." Apparently, a surgeon was on the way—from Banner Desert.

By that time, about twenty people were in Dale's ER "room"—a scrub team and ten friends. When the reluctant surgeon arrived, he threw back the curtain and said, "Mr. Knight. Mr. Knight! You've suffered a catastrophe, and you're going to die!"

No kidding.

Everyone was silent. For a moment, I thought he was joking. He wasn't. He literally said, "I'm not kidding. The only reason I'm here is because you're young and I'm going to give you a chance."

The ER doc told me later, "If I'd been standing next to him, I would've punched his lights out. But, Kim, we needed him."

Suddenly the scrub team jumped into action. With very little fanfare, they rolled Dale off to surgery. I'll always remember the funny little wave he gave on his way out. I thought they'd prep him and I'd get a chance to talk with him before they administered anesthesia, but that didn't happen. They'd been waiting so long for a surgeon that they took him straight to surgery.

My neighbor and good friend, Bill, said, "I don't believe that doctor. Dale is going to be fine." We prayed in the emergency room, our friends all expressed good wishes, and most people left. Bill, his wife, Christine, and several other friends went with me to a waiting area.

My mom called to see what was happening. She asked to talk to Bill and said, "Do *not* leave Kim there by herself. I'll be there tomorrow." Bill promised someone would stay with me, and Mom hung up.

Friends came and went for the next couple hours. A surgical nurse came out to tell me what was happening. "We had to lower Dale's body temperature in order to do surgery. We're just getting started."

"When will I get to talk to him?"

"Oh, you won't. We put him out a couple of hours ago."

I've thought a lot about what I might have said to my husband of twenty-two years. But, honestly, I'm glad I didn't get to have that conversation. If I'd had a chance to say those private thoughts, maybe he'd have been worried. I believe Dale's last thought was, *They're going to fix me right up.*

The surgery lasted for about eight hours. Finally, the surgeon who'd been so callous earlier came out to talk to me. I don't know if he'd thought about his initial remarks or if someone told him how awful he'd sounded, but he was much more kind now as he gave me an update on Dale's condition.

"Mrs. Knight, Mr. Knight is in recovery. I did the best I could, but I could only repair about one inch of his aorta. It was like working with tissue paper. He's stable, and I think his aorta will hold up. But swelling on his brain is likely to kill him."

My kids arrived before I had time to consider Dale's prognosis. I filled them in on what I knew, and I sent my neighbors home. My pastor, Allan, came out to talk with me after his meeting ended. We waited for Dale to leave recovery and to be taken to a room.

I sent everyone home except Erin. We waited to hear from the head of the Cardiovascular Intensive Care Unit (CVICU). A doctor about fifty years old—six years younger than Dale— came out to talk with us.

"Mrs. Knight, there isn't another person in this hospital in as much trouble as your husband. We need to talk about the amount of disability he'd be willing to live with."

"What amount of disability would you be willing to live with?"

"Almost none."

"I think that's where Dale would be too."

"Well, there is going to be some disability. He'll probably have some amount of paralysis, and he'll remain on a ventilator."

"Will he be able to talk?"

"Probably not."

I couldn't imagine it. My husband, the most interesting person I've ever met, the guy who made a living for thirty years as a salesman, wouldn't be able to walk or talk. He couldn't take it. I'm not sure I could either.

"You should go home and get some sleep."

"Oh no. I want to be here when he wakes up."

"Kim, he's not going to wake up."

"Not now or not ever?"

"Probably not ever."

All of this sounds cold but, honestly, I was truly grateful for the straight talk. At no time did I have any unfounded expectations about how this might turn out. The CVICU doc took Erin and me to another waiting room, and we finally got to see Dale for a few minutes. He was hooked up to a ventilator and some other machines and was totally unresponsive. My Dale would've had some wise remark about how he looked or where was the damn blazer. Where was the damn blazer, anyway? This Dale was a very sick man. I needed to get my head in the game.

When I got home, I sent out a few e-mails to tell everyone what was happening. I had to notify the company from which we'd just purchased the franchise. I knew no matter what the outcome, I wouldn't be able to continue with our plans. It wasn't a one-man operation, and I couldn't take care of Dale and run a business too. The franchise people were wonderful and told me to call when I was ready to make some decisions. Ultimately, they let me out of our agreement and returned our check. I'm eternally grateful to them for their kindness.

At about six in the morning, I received a phone call from the hospital. For a moment I thought, *Dale woke up!* But it was a different doctor, a neurologist, who said he was calling to ask me to authorize a DNR for Dale. I said I didn't know what that was.

"It's a 'do not resuscitate' order."

"What does that mean?"

"It means when we determine there's nothing else we can do for Dale, we won't use any special means to keep him alive."

"Please don't do anything yet! I'll be right there!"

"Mrs. Knight, Mr. Knight's left pupil is blown and we can't do anything else."

"I don't know what that means."

"It means his left pupil is fixed and dilated. I've been running a CT scan on Mr. Knight every half hour throughout the night, and there's a great deal of swelling in his brain. There's nothing we can do to relieve that. The only option would be to do a craniotomy, and he wouldn't survive that surgery this soon after open-heart surgery."

"I'll be right there!"

I jumped out of bed, got dressed, and asked Beau to pick up my mom when her flight arrived and come straight to the hospital. By the time I got back to the hospital, both of Dale's pupils were fixed and dilated; there was no brain activity.

Mom and the kids arrived. Mom's first remark was, "Can you believe this is happening to Dale so soon after it happened to your dad?" She was absolutely stricken, and I'll never forget the look on her face. Cole called to say he was about halfway to Phoenix. I prayed Dale would live until Cole arrived.

We went to Dale's room, and Pastor Allan met us there. He prayed with us and said he'd wait down the hall. I told him he didn't have to stay, but he said he'd be there if I wanted to talk. I'll be forever grateful for his presence that day.

The neurologist came back to explain there was no hope for

recovery. Dale would never wake up. We should disconnect the respirator.

Dale had been very well prepared for retirement and we did have wills; but we didn't have living wills, medical powers of attorney, or anything like that. I don't think we'd ever talked about what we'd want if we were ever in this situation. I wondered what his mom would think. I prayed Cole would come.

Cole did arrive and quickly saw how bad things were. He spent time with Dale privately, and I remember how grateful I was that he had come. It's funny the things you think about at times like this. We all told "Dale stories" about funny and meaningful times. We cried. We prayed. We talked about how it didn't seem real.

It was a devastating time, but I felt calm. Allan came down to sit with me and remarked on how calm I seemed.

"I know. Isn't it weird?" I replied. "I don't know if it's the 'peace that passes all understanding' or if it's the 'calm before the storm.' I think I'm in shock."

He answered some questions I had about what comes next and assured me I was making good decisions.

After we all had time to say our good-byes, the time came to *really* say good-bye. And in the course of a day, my husband, stepdad to my two children, business partner, best friend, and— truly—the most interesting person I have ever known, died.

 # *Your Story*

Have you lost your spouse, your parent, or a beloved friend? What is your story?

Did your spouse die suddenly or stay ill for some time?

If you were able to talk with your loved one shortly before their passing, what did you talk about? Did that provide some measure of closure for you?

How are you now? No, *really*.

2

What's the Password?

Wow! What just happened?

I sat with Dale for a while and thought about the events of the past day. Had it really only been a day? Yesterday we'd laughed about "Dale Knight Enterprises," and today Dale Knight was dead.

Cole, Beau, Meagan, and I spent some time making phone calls to people who needed to hear the news of Dale's passing from family. Word would get out soon enough through friends and neighbors.

It's really hard to call a mother to tell her that her son has died. It's just not the natural progression of life. Dale's mom had been informed as everything was happening, but it was heartbreaking to let her know Dale was gone. We talked a little about Dale's life and the details of his passing—which really had been peaceful. I told her I'd call her when we started making arrangements. She said she would probably not be able to come because she was still in the hospital. There was so much to say, yet so few words were adequate.

When I walked out of Dale's room, a hospital representative was waiting for me.

"Mrs. Knight, I'm so sorry to tell you this, but we don't have a morgue here at the hospital. You'll have to make arrangements to have Mr. Knight taken somewhere."

"When?"

"Right now."

Wow. Wow! Who do I call? Where do I start? I'm from a small town with one excellent mortuary. You know who to call. They know who you are. They know what to do.

"Who do I call?"

She handed me a list with names, phone numbers, addresses . . . prices. Prices.

"Do you know about any of these places?"

"A lot of people use Valley of the Sun. They're really big."

"Do they do a good job?"

"I don't really know. Please let me know when you make a decision."

"Do you know anything about organ donation? Could Dale be an organ donor?"

"No. Because of the way his organs shut down, you won't be able to donate his organs. Please let me know if you have any other questions. I'm so sorry, Mrs. Knight."

Reality. Right now.

Beau and Meagan were gathering Dale's things. The navy blazer safe on its hanger. The rest of the stuff still jammed in the bag. Where were his loafers? Is his watch in the bag?

I told Beau and Meagan about my conversation.

"Where do we start?"

Meagan started searching mortuaries on her phone. I called church to see if they could recommend someone.

Cindy answered the phone. "A lot of people use Valley of the Sun."

"That's what the hospital said."

"Our executive pastor has officiated many funerals there. I'll have him call them for you." All the teams I served on at church reported to him. I'd wait to hear from him.

Meagan researched the top five or six mortuaries on the list.

"The only one that has all good reviews is Bueler."

The miracle of the Internet. In five minutes, we narrowed down the list to two. Cindy called back. "Juno likes Valley of the Sun. He may be able to get you a better price because he works with them all the time."

Reality. Pricing. Are they available? Can they come right now?

It was getting late in the day, and I was worried they would close. I called Bueler first.

"Mrs. Knight, we're so sorry for your loss. Of course we can come for Mr. Knight. Please let the hospital know we're coming, and we'll call you when he's here. We can make plans for you to come over tomorrow."

I never called Valley of the Sun.

I had to fill out some forms. I asked one more time about organ donation. Someone came to reassure me that was not an option.

I wanted to go home.

In the car, one of Dale's best friends from Denver called. They'd worked together in the financial industry, and Ben ended up being Dale's manager. Ben was the one whose job it had been three months earlier to tell Dale his position had been eliminated. We knew his wife, Abbie. Erin babysat for his kids when we lived in Denver. Ben.

Abbie had told him Dale was in the hospital, so he called to see if he should come to Phoenix.

"Oh, Ben. Dale died." It was painful to say it out loud. It seemed so final.

"Died?"

"Just about an hour ago."

"He died?"

"I'm so sorry, Ben. You've been such a great friend."

"Oh my God. Oh my God. Oh my God!"

"I know. It doesn't seem real, does it?"

"You know, he told me to marry Abbie and I did."

"I know. He loved her too. Will you serve as a pallbearer?"

"We'll be there."

"I'll call you when I know what's happening."

I needed to call Pat—a good client who became a good friend. Dale and Pat's friendship had grown over the years through shared interests in cars, movies, World War II history, and attending men's Bible study at our previous church in Denver.

"Pat, I'm so sorry to let you know that Dale passed about an hour ago."

"Oh, Kim. I'm so sorry."

We reminisced about Dale. Pat, too, would serve as a pallbearer. "Linda and I are leaving for Phoenix as soon as possible. I'll tell our friends at church."

When I pulled into my driveway after leaving the hospital,

about ten neighbors were gathered there to welcome me home. We lived on the best street in the world with amazing neighbors who'd embraced us when we moved from Denver to Phoenix to start Dale's new job seven years ago. Amazing neighbors who sat in the driveway at Halloween to hand out candy and swap tales over drinks. Amazing neighbors who rented bouncy castles, had progressive dinners at Christmas, watched the Super Bowl, cheered on ASU and U of A. Amazing neighbors who were going to be there for the long haul.

We hugged and cried.

"What can we do?" they asked. "Can we bring food? Can we pick up people from the airport? Does anyone need to stay with you? Please call us. We're here for you."

I went inside. Two neighbors were organizing food and answering the phone. Flowers were everywhere. Beau and Meagan were making a list of people who had already brought things.

The doorbell rang, and it was my dentist carrying a huge floral arrangement. I had called his office when Dale entered the hospital to cancel Dale's appointment for the next day (the day he passed). We had to reschedule fairly often due to Dale's hectic travel schedule. The receptionist had kidded me, "Where's he going now?" She was shocked when I told her the news. To this day, his visit is an abiding reminder of how caring people have been.

We ate dinner and started getting ready for bed. Where should everyone sleep? The phone rang.

"Hi, Mrs. Knight! This is Sheila from the Organ Donor Network of Arizona. How are you doing today?"

Sheila was unbelievably perky.

"Truthfully, I've had better days."

"Well, we want to get paperwork started so that Mr. Knight can donate his organs."

Seriously? Seriously.

"The staff at the hospital told me Dale wouldn't be a candidate for organ donation."

"Who told you that?" Sheila's perkiness dissolved.

"I don't remember her name. Someone in the CVICU."

"That is *not* their decision to make. *We* make that decision."

"I asked twice, and the answer was the same each time."

"Well, you were misinformed. If we don't harvest Dale's organs within twenty-four hours, we won't be able to use them."

"Sheila, Dale is no longer at the hospital. He's been transported to Bueler Mortuary. They're probably closed by now."

"Well, our window of opportunity is closing."

"I'm sorry. That's all I know. I'm hanging up now."

I'll never forget that phone call—a cruel end to an awful day.

The next day, Bueler called to let me know Dale was there. Did I want to make an appointment to discuss Dale's arrangements? Please bring the clothing you'd like for him to wear. Beau, Erin, Cole and I went over that day. We took the navy blazer.

The people were absolutely wonderful. Bueler is a small family-owned facility, and it felt like it could've been in my small home-town. I'm truly grateful Meagan found them. It was the right place for Dale.

There were a lot of decisions to make. Where will the service be? What day? Traditional burial? Cremation? Flowers? Pricing became a reality. Bueler told me to order twenty death certificates. Twenty? Twenty. I was going to have to provide them to our bank, our investment accounts, Dale's life insurance provider, social security, and a number of other people. I had no idea. At a time when I would've preferred to get in bed and pull the covers over my head, I needed to get my head in the game.

When it had become apparent that Dale would not survive, Cole, Pastor Allan, and I had discussed cremation. I'm claustrophobic and I definitely want to be cremated, but Dale and I had never discussed it. Allan assured me our faith had no doctrine against cremation. I called Dale's mom and sister to ask if they'd give their blessing for Dale to be cremated. Both agreed. We discussed those arrangements with Bueler. We chose a casket. Dale was a big guy. You never think about caskets coming in sizes—but they do.

My daughter is a professional singer, and she agreed to sing at the service. She started looking up music on her phone.

Music! The only thing Dale and I had ever discussed about funeral arrangements was how he'd like to have a bagpiper play "Amazing Grace." Did Bueler know a bagpiper? No. Erin searched "bagpiper Phoenix AZ." She called several and found one who was available and who knew "Amazing Grace." Done.

We looked at urns. I couldn't imagine Dale resting in one of those formal urns. One option was a beautiful inlaid box and it looked . . . normal. Beau said, "It looks like a humidor."

That's it! Dale had occasionally smoked cigars, and he had a beautiful humidor. I would use a humidor. I couldn't use his because it was the wrong size. Later I went to purchase one at his cigar store. That's a story for another day, but—needless to say—it was an interesting conversation.

We made all of the necessary decisions, chose some music, went to the nearby florist.

Then everyone went home, but I went to church to discuss arrangements for Dale's memorial service. Dale and I had found Mountain Park Community Church when we moved to Phoenix in 2006, and we'd been very active there. I served on the women's team; Dale was active with the men's ministry. We started the greeter team with our small group. I ran the career ministry team. Eventually, I was asked to serve on the Board of Servant Leaders. It was our church home.

What do you do if you don't have a faith walk or a church to turn to in times like these? No judgment—just an observation. What's it like to have to make plans at a strange place with people you don't know? It must add an extra layer of sadness to a heartbreaking situation.

I am forever grateful I was sitting at a table with two women I knew well and loved: Cindy and Barb. We cried. I told them the whole story. We cried some more.

"It just doesn't seem real, Kim. You seem so calm."

We decided to have Dale's Celebration of Life on Saturday at five. That would allow time for the people who had to travel to get there. There were more decisions to make: Who'll serve as pallbearers? You need to call them. What music would you like? Erin will sing. Allan will do the service. Who else will speak? Beau and Erin will offer the eulogy. What's the order of the service? Will you do the program? Can I have a reception here at church?

I'd called around to see if one of our favorite restaurants would host some type of reception after the service. Nothing nearby was available. MPCC agreed to host the event, and a church member would cater it for me.

I asked if it would be okay if I parked Dale's sports car in front of the church for the service. When my dad had died a couple of years before, we'd brought his golf cart to the funeral home and parked it in the lobby. Dad had been an avid golfer, and people had loved it. It had been a memorable moment, and I wanted to do something similar for Dale. Cindy asked. It would be fine.

After a couple of hours, all the decisions were made. On the way home, I stopped by the bank where Dale had suffered his aneurysm. I told the manager who I was, and I asked to speak to the banker Dale had been meeting. I wanted to know what happened. Had Dale been afraid? Did it happen quickly? Who called the ambulance? I needed to fill in the parts of the story I hadn't heard. The banker wasn't there, but the banker who'd been in the next cubicle came out to talk with me. He told me what he knew.

"How is Mr. Knight doing?"

It was the first time I had to explain the situation to someone who didn't really know Dale. It's hard to tell the story without making the other person feel uncomfortable. I'm still working on it.

Later, Justin, the banker who'd called the ambulance for Dale, called me.

"Mrs. Knight, I'm so sorry to learn about Mr. Knight. One of your neighbors was in yesterday and told me he died." Justin told me Dale had only been there for a few minutes, and he'd been telling Justin about our new business. "Mrs. Knight, I want you to know Mr. Knight was so excited about it! He said you'd worked for him all these years and he was going to buy a business for you to run. He was going to work for you now. It was so cool to see how excited he was."

Apparently, Dale had been trying unsuccessfully to put a pen in the inside pocket of his blazer and had seemed a little disoriented. Justin asked him if he was okay. Dale didn't respond.

"Mr. Knight, I'm going to call your wife."

"What are you going to call her? . . . That's a joke!"

So Dale. He was still in there. Justin had called an ambulance and then called me.

"Mrs. Knight, please let me know if we can do anything for you. I'm so sorry."

I went home to find my mom sitting in the den with a very attractive man I didn't know.

"Kimbo, this is Frank. He's works with Annie."

Annie was in the investment business, and she and her husband were longtime friends of ours in Denver. She was unable to come to Phoenix for Dale's service so she'd sent Frank, who worked for her in Scottsdale, to convey her condolences with a framed picture from a trip we'd taken to Mexico and a bottle of tequila. Annie. Perfect.

Frank visited for a while and left.

I turned to my mom. "You let a total stranger into my home?"

"He was so handsome, I was willing to chance it!"

I hear you, Mom. Take your joy where you can find it.

I went to look for the keys to Dale's Shelby Cobra replica. He'd purchased the car about eight years before—the only frivolous thing he ever did. Royal blue with wide white stripes and Dale's pride and joy. I'd never driven it. I wasn't sure I knew how to start it. Where were the keys? Not in his desk. Not in the car. I looked in his nightstand. Bingo!

Dale was very organized and the drawer of his nightstand

was immaculate—a small tray of change, his Bible, car keys, and
. . . *what is that?* I picked up a small object made of wood and
plastic. *What is this? Oh my gosh! It's a hash pipe! Dale has drug
paraphernalia next to his Bible?* Dale had probably smoked a little
marijuana in his college days, and I'm pretty sure he would've
inhaled. But in all of our married life he'd never done drugs.
Why did he have a pipe? Where did he put in the drugs? How
does it work?

I looked down the "barrel" of the pipe and saw a reed. Like a
saxophone reed. *What is this thing? Oh my goodness! It's a duck call!*
I laughed until I cried. The duck call is now in *my* nightstand
next to *my* Bible. It's a great reminder of the absurdities of life.

Okay. Car keys. I went out to the garage and got into the car.
I tried to remember how Dale started the car. There's the fuel
switch. That's the choke. Turn on the fuel. Pull out the choke?
Push in the choke? I called Beau and Cole to help me. No luck.
The car wouldn't start. We called a neighbor to come down to
look. No luck.

I called Gary, Dale's longtime friend and car guy who was
going to serve as a pallbearer, to ask what I was doing wrong.

"Dale couldn't get it started last time he tried, either. Something must be wrong with the fuel pump."

Okay. No Cobra. Moving on.

Where were our wills? Did Dale have anything written down
about what he wanted for his funeral? Did he have a copy of his
life insurance policy? Where did he keep it?

I looked through our files and found a copy of Dale's life
insurance policy and my will but not Dale's. *Where would he have
put it? In the safe?* I found our little safe. *Where's the key?* Beau

came to help me, and we finally pried open the safe with some other key. Dale's will was there—with all of the normal formalities but no instructions about final wishes.

I'd worked for Dale for nearly twenty years. On a daily basis, I knew where he was, who he was meeting, and what he was saying. We had a wonderful working relationship, a great marriage and friendship, and spent a lot of time together. So it came as a huge shock to me that I didn't know anything about his passwords, how to start his car, how to take care of the pool, how to give the dog a bath, how to turn on the sprinklers, if he wanted to be cremated . . . or a thousand other things. These things weren't secrets. It just never occurred to me that I'd ever need to know them. He didn't know my passwords either. Why would he need to know?

Dale had a huge library of songs he'd purchased from iTunes on my computer. One of his hobbies was making CDs to give to friends when we visited them, to take on a trip, or to celebrate a special occasion. I wanted to put together a playlist of Dale's favorite songs to play during the visitation before his service, but I couldn't use the password-protected songs because I didn't know his iTunes password. I still haven't figured it out. I've never been into his personal e-mail for the same reason.

I learned by chance that Dale had opened an online investment account just before he died. The investment company sent something via snail mail, and I learned about the stock he'd gotten as part of his severance package. I used one of Dale's twenty death certificates to gain access to that account.

When my dad died, hundreds of people came to his service. He'd been a well-known businessman and a renowned golfer.

After Dad's service, Dale had said, "That was really impressive. I can't believe how many people came. I don't think hundreds of people would come to my service."

So Dale would've been shocked and delighted to see the hundreds of people who did stand in line for hours to pay their condolences at his Celebration of Life. Family, friends, and coworkers came from Colorado, California, Illinois, Missouri, Texas, and Arizona. Clients spent their Saturday driving in from all over the region to pay their respects.

Beau and Dale's niece welcomed our friends and family; Beau and Erin offered the eulogy; Allan did a beautiful, personal reflection on Dale's life; other friends shared memories; Erin, Beau, and a gospel choir sang; and eight fine men served as pallbearers. At the appointed time, I turned to see the bagpiper walking down the side aisle to lead Dale out to the strains of "Amazing Grace." He looked perfect—white hair and mustache, kilt, glengarry hat, knee socks, and sporran pouch. Later, we all had to laugh that maybe he didn't actually *know* "Amazing Grace"—but it was a memorable exit for an amazing man.

I couldn't send Dale off without a Jack Daniel's toast over a cigar, so we adjourned to my house after the reception. Probably a hundred friends and neighbors came over to tell funny Dale stories and to smoke cigars from Dale's humidor. You should've seen the food—it looked like New Year's Eve! Everything was perfect except that Dale wasn't there. He would've loved it.

The evening finally came to an end. I looked at all the food we had left over and said, "Well, clearly we don't need more food, but I could use another refrigerator." Within five minutes, four neighbors went up the street, put an unused fridge on a dolly, and rolled it down to my house. No problem. Dale would have howled!

Throughout the next day, our friends dropped by to say their good-byes as they left town. We packaged up leftovers, made "to-go" boxes, hugged, cried, and sent them on their way. Eventually my mom, Cole, Erin, Beau, and Meagan had to go home too.

Life without Dale began.

 # Your Story

When did life without your spouse begin?

Were your children still living at home? How old were they? Were you still working?

What was the hardest thing to deal with? Has it gotten easier with time?

What is your happiest memory of that time?

Who was your biggest supporter? Did you let them know? It's not too late.

Was anyone difficult? Have you forgiven them?

3

Life Changes ...
Over Time

The day after Dale's Celebration of Life, our friends Bob and Sandy celebrated their daughter's wedding. Sandy ran the children's ministry at church. Bob served on the drama team. Bob and Dale had bonded over a shared love of The Who.

Bob and Sandy were living under a cloud because Sandy had been diagnosed with ovarian/uterine cancer the year before. She'd had some encouraging results, and they were hopeful for a good outcome. Then Sandy suffered a stroke at church the following Easter. That's when Bob began to doubt that Sandy would recover.

Bob wore his "best actor face" for public life. He wanted his faith walk to be evident to those who knew him, but it took a huge toll on his mental health to live two different sets of emotions. Bob admitted that when people told him he was "so strong," he wanted to say, "Do you have any idea how empty I feel? I've been running on empty for two years."

When Bob realized it was not going to end well, he started

his grieving process—and felt guilty. He began to live as if he were going through Sandy's last days—and felt guilty. He said, "Life as we knew it was over with her diagnosis. I mourned the changes in our marriage. I mourned the changes in her. I put on my best actor face because I didn't want my daughters to know that something was terribly wrong with their mom." Bob and Sandy answered their daughters' questions when asked but didn't volunteer information. They wanted to spare them as much worry as possible. Their older daughter was expecting their first grandchild, and they wanted her pregnancy to be as free from stress as possible. Bob prayed, *Oh God, please don't let it feel like this for the rest of Sandy's life.*

Six months after Dale died, Sandy was taken to hospice. She didn't want to go but had become too ill to continue her care at home. Bob told me later, "If she had died at home under my care, I would have felt like I killed her." What terrible guilt to live with! Sandy was transported to hospice care and died after being in her room for only five minutes. Bob felt relief after she died because her suffering was over. Then he felt guilty about feeling relieved.

When I asked Bob if he had any regrets, he said, "I should have requested a caregiver so I could've just been a husband. I wish someone had taken care of both of us for a few days. And I'll always wonder if I did everything I could."

Because we intended for people to think we were handling everything well, Bob and I became the faces of a club that no one wants to join. Friends who knew friends struggling with loss asked us (separately) to counsel them. Just when our emotional reserves were running dry, we put on our "perfect widow masks" and ministered to those hurting souls. It's gut wrenching and exhausting.

My aunt and uncle lived a different kind of loss. George was a retired Illinois state trooper—a big, handsome guy with a heart of gold. LaVerne was a sweetheart—quiet and pretty, a great companion for my uncle. She was diagnosed with Alzheimer's disease back before you heard much about it. At first, LaVerne just seemed a little forgetful, then her progressing symptoms led to the devastating diagnosis. George took care of her at home for as long as he could. His generation didn't turn over care to an outsider easily. He finally had to find help when it became dangerous for her to stay home alone.

George never would have said how difficult it was to provide care for someone who didn't know who he was all the time. But if you've lived this story, you know how heartbreaking it is. LaVerne became increasingly agitated and suspicious. If George left to go to the grocery store, she thought he was going to meet his "girlfriend." Eventually, she needed to be in an assisted memory care facility. George would go out to visit LaVerne at mealtime—every meal, every day. In the evening, they would share a Hershey's bar. He never complained about his special kind of loss. LaVerne did well physically for many years, but it was a crushing blow for the entire family to watch her lose her memories, their shared history. She would've been mortified at the changes that took place in her personality over the final years.

George loved to dance, and—when LaVerne could no longer go—once a month he would go to the dance at the local lodge. Our family thought it was great that he had an outlet for relief from his caregiver role. One evening, a well-meaning friend said that "it just didn't look right" for George to be out dancing while his wife was in a nursing home. He never went again. George was diagnosed with colon cancer shortly after LaVerne died and survived only two weeks.

Did you know widowhood increases the surviving spouse's risk of dying? Sixty percent of those who lose a spouse or significant other will experience a serious illness in the twelve months following that loss.[1] This can be partially attributed to the death of a spouse being ranked as the number one stressor on the Holmes and Rahe stress scale, making it one of life's most devastating events.[2]

If your spouse experienced a long illness, you may be able to relate to the conflicting emotions that come with the experience. Did you transition from loving spouse to faithful caregiver? Did you feel guilty about feeling relieved? Were you, too, running on empty? Many of the people I approached to share their caregiver stories chose not to participate. Most said they just didn't want to relive that time in their lives. They were trying to move beyond it, and it would have been too difficult to think about it again.

I did talk with Larry, who lost his wife to cancer. Their sixtieth wedding anniversary would've been a week after our conversation. Larry shared a lot of beautiful memories about Carol, but when it came time to talk about her last days, he just couldn't do it. He was able to tell me that his sister came to help for the last couple of weeks and that he told Carol, "It's time to go," but he absolutely couldn't discuss his distress over the events. His emotions were now devoted to his dog, his sons, and his grandchildren.

As I compiled stories for this book, I asked those widows whose spouses had been ill for some time if they thought it would've been better if their loved one had passed suddenly. For those whose spouse died from a sudden event, I asked if they wished their loved one could have passed after a prolonged illness. Interestingly enough, every single person chose the road they traveled. Including me. Just coincidence? Or did God in His wisdom allow the right path?

Your Story

How did caring for your ailing spouse change your marriage?

What things did you miss the most when you were caring for your spouse?

How did your friends and family react during this time?

Did you put on your brave face for the outside world?

Have you taken on the role of counselor to other widows in your circle of friends?

Who was most helpful to you at this time? What did they do that impacted you in a positive way?

In what ways do you feel the mourning process changes when you have a chance to deal with the loss of your spouse before their actual death?

If you could change anything about the loss of your spouse, what would it be?

4

When the Casserole Days Are Over

If you've read this far, perhaps your own life—or that of someone you love—took a path similar to the first chapters. Please know you're not walking this road alone. But at this stage, you may be pondering how life changed so quickly and how you might move forward from wherever you are. I totally hear you.

Within a week of Dale's death, real life marched on. The water pipe from the street to our home burst under the driveway. Our two air-conditioning units failed. The mortgage had to be paid. My daughter, Erin, had some health problems, and I relocated to Denver for a month to help care for her.

By the time I returned to Phoenix, life had returned to normal for nearly everyone. When I ran into friends and neighbors in the community, everyone was still friendly and solicitous.

"How are you? Can we do anything for you? Do you need help with anything at the house? Please come to dinner."

I'd worked for Dale as his administrative assistant for the past twenty years. When he was restructured out of his job, we planned to buy a franchise and work for another five or ten years. Now the office—his office—was empty. I wasn't working. Bible study was over for the summer. It was hot, and neighbors were staying inside. For the first time in my adult life, I felt lonely.

Throughout our married life, Dale traveled for business five days a week, forty-eight weeks a year. I'd spent a lot of time alone—but I'd never been lonely. I raised my children, worked, volunteered at school, went out with friends, traveled. Dale called me twenty times a day to discuss business: "What time is my next appointment? Did you make reservations for lunch? Can you make my travel arrangements for next week? What does my week look like?" Sometimes I had to roll my eyes, he called so often. Frequently, the conversation started with, "I know I'm driving you crazy, but . . ." What I wouldn't give for one of those phone calls now.

I spent time writing thank-you notes—hundreds of them. I learned how to clean my pool. I pulled the first mouse from my pool sweep. I paid bills. I walked my dog, Weston. I got my finances in order. I used most of the twenty death certificates to change our investment accounts over to my name. I traded in Dale's Chrysler and my fourteen-year-old Jeep for a Ford Explorer. I celebrated my birthday and cried over his.

Now what? Maybe you've asked this question too.

I've never been a "tragic figure," and I did not intend to become one now. But I really struggled with the "So now what?" question. I accepted all social invitations. I tried to embrace my "new normal." Beau and Meagan left. Mom went home. Erin recovered. My friends returned to work. I felt lonely. I felt married. I have never known such sorrow.

My friends, family, neighbors, and church family has been absolutely amazing from the first moments of Dale entering the hospital until now. I hope you've had a wonderful support system too. But, eventually, everyone gets to go back to real life—except for you.

The harsh reality is that everyone else is dealing with something too. Poor health. Bad marriages. Divorce. Aging parents. Troubled kids. Money. Career. Death. It's easy to think that you're alone in your grief because everyone else is dealing with their own heartaches. Eventually, even the death of a great friend and neighbor fades to yesterday's news.

My kids lost their devoted stepdad, but they still had their dad. They still had me. My friends and neighbors had struggles of their own. My mom ran her own business in a town fifteen hundred miles away. My church was transitioning to a new system of courses and Bible studies. I recently saw a Robert Frost quote that totally summarized my feelings: "In three words I can sum up everything I've learned about life: It goes on." Indeed.

My neighbor Christine "adopted" me. Every night that she cooked, she invited me to dinner. Weston and I would stop by after our walk and eat. We'd sit outside and talk about how hot it was. We'd get in the pool and solve the world's problems.

Her husband would join us for dinner and then retreat to his office. Dale and Bill had been very close friends—"two of a kind," Christine and I always said. Traveling salesmen with brilliant minds and strong opinions. After Dale died, Bill—a close friend to both of us—no longer spent much time with me because it reminded him of Dale. Though his loss was different from mine, Dale's death was personal and intense for Bill, too.

He lost the "best friend he ever had," a kindred spirit, an equal who lived down the street.

More than two years after Dale died, I talked with Gary, Dale's dear friend and business associate, about the changes in our relationship. Gary and his wife, Pam, were longtime friends who enjoyed similar pursuits. We'd been to several car races together and went on long Sunday drives to our favorite Mexican restaurants. Both worked in the investment industry with Dale.

We hadn't seen each other since Dale's funeral, and I wondered if we were still friends. Gary said, "You know, it really wouldn't have been appropriate for me to call you to do stuff after Dale died." Simple truth that made complete sense. Pam still checked in, though, and it was great to catch up with Gary in person. It felt like "old times."

Gary stopped going to car races because it wasn't the same without Dale. His death was so shocking that it's still a topic of conversation among their friends. It made them think about their own mortality. Pam and Gary shared their regret that we planned to meet after the holidays but never scheduled anything. Then Dale died. As Buddha said, "The trouble is, you think you have time."

My mom also experienced the loss of several good friends when my dad died. She and Dad used to have lunch every day with one of their friends. After Dad died, that friend served as a pallbearer and then quit calling. Chester is a small town with few options for lunch. Truthfully, he would've had to go out of his way *not* to talk with my mom, but he just dropped out of sight. My mom called one day to tell me that he called to take her to lunch—three years after my dad died.

Two other couples dropped out too. Mom and Dad had known them for years; they traveled together, went to the movies, talked on a daily basis. But after Dad's death, they stopped calling. They each sent a Christmas card this year and said they needed to get together—again, three years after Dad died. One couple wrote a long letter confessing they had failed Mom, but they just couldn't deal with his death. It made them feel old and mortal. If a guy as young and vital as Dad could die, that meant they could too.

Would you be shocked to learn that, on average, 75 percent of the survivor's support base is lost following the loss of a spouse or significant other?[1] There are many reasons why this might be true: moving to a new place, loss of "couples friends," having a despondent outlook, grief on the part of family and friends. This loss of support base can be especially difficult for the survivor who lost a spouse to suicide. They may feel so socially isolated and ashamed that they dread facing their acquaintances in the community.

If your friends' grief changed your relationships after your spouse died, it doesn't mean that they didn't really care about you. The way they chose to deal with the death of someone they loved was just different. We can analyze why they dropped out forever, but the short story is it wasn't dislike for you. It was love for your spouse. And the price of that love is grief.

Christine called me one day to ask me to dinner on the upcoming Saturday. I told her I'd love to come and asked what I could bring. "Nothing," she said. "I'm having couples over on Friday and I'm prepping for both nights."

"Thanks so much! I'd love to come," I said. But I thought,

Couples. I'm not a couple. I'm not coming on Friday. I'm coming on Saturday.

We hung up, and I considered my new status as not half a couple. One minute later, the phone rang. It was Christine.

"I don't know why I said that. Of course you are welcome to come on Friday. What was I thinking?"

I assured her no harm was done and said I couldn't come on Friday anyway. "I'll see you on Saturday."

Christine and the rest of my neighbors have never treated me like I wasn't welcome. I've since been to many "couples" dinner parties as a single, and I've had lots of couples to my home. But I have changed my thinking about two things: how I feel when I'm included in a gathering of couples, and how I think about singles in my social circle.

The first one is that being included as a single at a couples' party makes me feel like things haven't changed. It makes me feel wanted and included in neighborhood events. But the ironic part about being included is leaving that group of couples to go home alone at the end of the evening emphasizes that—indeed—I am no longer half a couple.

Some widowed friends have shared that I should be glad I'm still included in groups of couples because they were removed from that invitation list. So, just when we need to be around friends, our social lives take a hit too.

I recently talked with Pat, who'd been widowed for just a few months when she went on a short trip with a tour group composed primarily of couples to see how she'd feel about traveling alone. She had a great first day and returned to her room alone only to have a full-on meltdown. "I totally lost it." She said.

"Going back to that hotel room by myself was more than I could bear. I wanted to tell my husband about my day and to ask about his; but he wasn't there. I nearly left for home after one day."

My golfing buddy, Marilyn, told me that when her husband died suddenly, she lost not only her husband but his adult children, too. After Mickey's funeral, they quit making an effort to get together. She went from being a wife and stepmother of more than fifty years to single and alone—almost overnight.

Susan, widowed when her husband was killed in Iraq, talked about attending a military ball at the nearby base. She loved to go because it made her feel like she was still part of her military family. However, sitting at the table watching all of the couples dancing was heartbreaking. It solidified her "aloneness"—mentioned by nearly every widowed person as the most gut-wrenching part of losing a spouse.

Larry moved from Las Vegas to Phoenix to be near one of his sons, but he missed his life in Las Vegas. Many people I spoke to moved to be near their children but left their "real lives" behind. At a time when a support system is vital to recovery, many widows move away from all they've ever known. While it may seem logical to relocate nearer to family, there may be unexpected "fallout" from such a move. One woman admitted that after moving in with her daughter, the daughter took over her life. She knew her daughter did it out of love and concern, but she was mentally and financially sound and wanted her life back.

Another friend who sells real estate experienced a very different and difficult transition. She was diagnosed with macular degeneration about the time her husband was diagnosed with lung cancer, suffered a short illness, and died. Her driving privileges were suspended due to her vision challenges, and she became dependent upon others for her transportation. Within a short time, she lost her husband, her ability to drive, her job, a significant source of income, and a great deal of her independence. Heartbreaking!

The second change in my thinking is how I think about singles. I mentioned some thoughts about living as a single person to my never-married friend and neighbor, Lyn, who said, "Now you know how I feel."

Her words stung because I'd been guilty of not including Lyn when Dale and I had couples over. I always had plenty of food and I could certainly make room for one more, but I didn't think to ask her. Lyn was included when the girls came, when the neighborhood had a party, and when we went out one-on-one. But it had never occurred to me to have her come with couples. Now I was in her shoes, and the reality of my decision confronted me. I won't make that mistake in the future.

Even at church—where I knew nearly everyone—I felt alone. I still went every Sunday. I was on the greeter team. I was expected. The "perfect widow" would show up—so I did.

One of my favorite radio talk show hosts does a "Happiness Hour" on Fridays, which is a serious look at the importance of being happy. I decided to embrace some of his suggestions to promote happiness within myself. One is that you have an obligation to act happy—even if you're not—for the benefit of the people around you. And if you *act* happy, eventually you will *be* happier. If you walk around in gloom, you will make the people around you unhappy and the time will come that they will not want to be around you. I knew for sure I did not want to be *that* person. And after a year of wearing my perfect widow mask, I *was* happier. Genuinely happier.

After Lyn was diagnosed with cancer, she put on her brave cancer mask about the same time as I took up the role of the perfect widow. We ran into each other one day when Weston and I were circling the block.

I asked her how she was doing, and she said, "I'm okay. I just bought a new convertible. I decided I'm going to put the top down and let the wind blow through my hair while I still have hair. You should go do fun stuff while you can, Kim."

God bless you, Lyn! It was her version of "If life gives you lemons . . ." and she made me realize how many blessings I had. I needed to "get over myself."

Though our spouses encountered death, currently we are alive. Lyn was a single friend who had never been in a marital relationship and who was facing a tough battle with cancer, which she has since lost. But she decided to let the wind blow through her hair with wild abandon. You go, girl! I'm in!

 # Your Story

How have your relationships with friends changed since your spouse died?

What happened? When did you notice?

What have you done to reconnect with friends you haven't seen in a while?

How did they respond?

What does your circle of friends look like now?

What have you done to meet new friends?

5

What's in His Pockets?

After Dale died, I needed to "get my ducks in a row." He'd been thorough, so I knew everything I needed to know was in the office somewhere. I just needed to go through his files to see what was there.

I was about halfway through the first file drawer when I stopped. *What if I find something I don't want to know?* I was looking through folders, travel plans, pictures, receipts—fifty-six years of memories, planning, life. *Oh please, Jesus. Don't let me find anything that changes the way I view my marriage.*

Halfway through the second file drawer, I stopped again. What's this? I opened a folder filled with cards and letters to Dale from me. Twenty-six years of Father's Days, anniversaries, love notes, birthday cards, "just because" notes. Tears rolled down my face. *He* had saved them. All of them. These weren't letters I stashed away. *He* kept them. We moved and *he* moved them. I read through every memory and put them back in the folder. I would move them next time.

In all, I found one duck call, one pile of love letters, one of my leather jackets in the trunk of his car, and one pair of Elvis sunglasses complete with fake sideburns in a coat pocket. I can't tell you how relieved I was *not* to discover anything I didn't want to know.

But what if you did? How do you move forward?

You would be shocked to hear some of the things people learned about their husband after his death—cancelled life insurance policies, substance abuse, extramarital affairs, other children, sexual abuse, serious money issues. Many secrets were revealed immediately after the funeral. Spouses and children started going through their relative's personal, private belongings and correspondence and discovered things. People had literally been waiting for someone to die to finally talk about the "issue."

In researching how to acknowledge and deal with this sensitive subject, I found not much has been written. As one writer put it, "How do you research people who are keeping secrets?"[1]

Once the "genie is out of the bottle," it's rare for people to just move on. Usually, that's just the beginning of uncovering the whole truth—some of which you may not really want to know. In this information age, it's fairly easy to research facts through the Internet, Ancestry.com, courthouse records, extended family, and friends. Access to e-mail, texts, diaries, and correspondence might provide additional information.

Evan Imber-Black, author of *The Secret Life of Families*, reminds us that once you unearth one secret, you might find that more secrets just keep coming. "For some families, it's just the way they do business."[2]

If you do follow the story through to its conclusion, then what? Who do you tell? What are the consequences? Is it worth impacting other relationships? Are you looking for healing, or are you looking to punish your spouse?

A dear friend, Victoria, found out her husband of thirty-three years was gay. He didn't die, but he left the marriage and moved to another city to begin a new career and embrace a new life. Victoria and I traveled together shortly after her husband left, and we spent hours discussing the similarities and differences between our two stories.

Grieving the death of your spouse is a soul-baring, excruciatingly painful process that will likely go on for years. But failing to move forward isn't really an option for most of us. The reality is that your spouse is never coming back.

Grieving the loss of her marriage was extraordinarily painful for Victoria for different reasons. One is that Victoria and her husband were not planning to share the primary reason he was leaving with most people. So it was hard to process her "new normal"—especially in public. At least when your spouse dies, people know. I asked Victoria what life would have been like if she had found out about her husband after he died instead of before he left. She wrote:

> I totally agree about it being easier to find out about him now, when I can still talk to him and figure things out. Finding out after he died would feel like I would never get out of limbo land! Awful, awful. I'd feel as though I couldn't embrace any part of my past with joy because I'd never know if any part of it was real. Now, at least

I can recognize that parts of my marriage were real and wonderful and worth holding on to—and that there are other parts I will hold a bit more loosely and now view with a different perspective.

We also discussed the frustration that comes with not being able to control the situation in which you find yourself. When Victoria's husband decided to reveal his secret to her, it wasn't to get her opinion on what should happen next. It was to leave the marriage and to move forward on his own—without her. When your spouse died, you had no choice in the matter. However, there are two major differences: Victoria's husband chose to leave, but—in most cases—your spouse did not. Victoria could still talk with her husband, and he was still alive to be longed for—with no chance of ever reciprocating her feelings. Actually talking with a deceased spouse is no longer an option. But while we still long for the marriage relationship, most of us don't feel abandoned. Both spouses are unattainable for uniquely different reasons.

My friend Mary had a similar experience when her husband died. When I asked her how she was doing, she said, "You know, I started grieving my marriage when my husband had an affair many years ago. He chose to leave our marriage then, but he didn't choose to die now." Though she was alone now, she didn't feel abandoned.

So what if you did find out something about your husband or marriage you didn't want to know?

Because I didn't live this scenario, I'm not sure how I would react. But I think I would revisit nearly every aspect of my life with my spouse to see if I could see the beginnings of the deception—like rewinding a movie to see if you can spot the foreshadowing.

What should we do? Dig through every nook and cranny to see what else we might find? Should we track down the people who know answers to our questions? Hire a professional to help?

Now, is that healthy? Maybe not. Human? Yes. Is there a more rational approach? Probably. But how do we get there? Given my nature to track the answer until I'm satisfied, I wasn't sure, so—don't laugh—I searched "How to Deal with Bad News" on WikiHow.com![3]

The first suggestion was: "Don't hold back your emotions and don't try to act brave." Speaking as the "perfect widow," I can attest to the fact that this is exhausting. I found I was living two sets of emotions—one for public consumption and the *real* one. Double the effort on half the energy. Accept that you're going to have a few screaming, rip-your-hair-out moments—and then you'll start to feel better. Trying to hold it all in will make your heart and head explode.

Then, don't feel guilty. Ah . . . guilt rears its ugly head. Why do we always blame ourselves first? In all likelihood, if you didn't even *know* what your spouse was hiding, it is *not* your fault. You're also not allowed to feel guilty for not knowing. *You didn't know.* More than one researcher observed that the secret tells far more about the secret *keeper* than the person who has learned the secret.

Look at the bright side. And there always is one. Warning: this may take some time and closer evaluation. It's easy to assume "Eeyore mode." If you don't know who Eeyore is and why this is bad, stop reading now and pick up *Winnie the Pooh*. After *Winnie*, make a list of the good things in your life. Put your list where you can read it. Read it often. Read it out loud. Repeat.

Distract yourself: Try some retail therapy, work a puzzle, go to a movie, read a book, take a walk. This might be a great time to read the classics, learn to knit, take up chess or bridge—totally mystifying games that will occupy your mind. Anytime you're thinking about something else, you're not thinking about this.

Understand what is going on. Find out as much as you can. I liked this suggestion as it feeds into my crazy fact-finder side, as described above. But, seriously, collect as much *factual* information as possible. Try to leave the rumors and innuendo for another time.

Talk the news through. Share your anger, sorrow, feelings, and heartache with someone else. Maybe a friend. Maybe a professional. Maybe God. Probably not your children or his mother. But—at some point—you have to let it go and give yourself permission to move forward.

Know that you are not alone. While it may feel like you are the only person on earth who has ever felt this way, you aren't. Life isn't going to be easy, but it won't always be this hard either. And whether we like to admit it or not, the passage of time really does diminish the pain.

If you have a faith walk—and even if you don't—maybe this is something you can hand over to God. Tell Him how you feel. Ask Him to help you move past this. If you've never spoken to God before, now is a perfect time to start. But how do you begin? Find a quiet place, close your eyes, and start talking—there aren't any rules for prayer. You'll be amazed to learn that God is a good listener and He will meet you where you are.

Please don't let whatever you've learned keep you from moving ahead and reclaiming your life. What a shame to be held captive by something that happened a long time ago, without your knowledge, and over which you had no control. At some point, you have to put one foot in front of the other. And. Move. Forward.

 # Your Story

How long did you wait before you went through your spouse's personal belongings?

If you haven't gone through his/her things yet, what keeps you from starting? Which trusted friends can help?

Share the best thing you discovered that you didn't already know.

What did you discover that you wish you hadn't found?

How did learning something unknown make you feel?

Describe how it changed your feelings about your marriage.

What did you do with the information? Were you able to let it go? Who did you tell? What were the consequences?

6

Where Was God When I Needed Him?

My friend Margie and her husband, Jim, were in the emergency room before Dale went into surgery. They'd been in our small group Bible study, called Knights' Roundtable Discussion, since it began. Jim was our fact-checker, Margie our prayer warrior.

Years ago, Dale had sleep apnea surgery that didn't go well. He had to go back in for additional surgery the same day after "coding" in his hospital room. Dale ended up in the ICU for a week before he was able to go home. It was pretty traumatic for all concerned.

While Dale was still in the ICU, Margie sent me an e-mail that read: *I'm still praying for you and Dale. I felt like I needed to send you this verse: "'For I know the plans I have for you,' declares the Lord, 'plans to prosper you and not to harm you, plans to give you hope and a future'" (Jeremiah 29:11).*

I'd never had a "life verse" until that moment, but I've held tight to that verse ever since. It was written to the people of Israel when they were in captivity. It serves as a reminder that

God knows my future and I shouldn't waste my years even if I'm in "captivity" of some kind.

Dale's Aunt Mildred lives in Georgia. After Dale died, I received a large package from her. Inside was a lovely note telling me how sorry she was to learn about Dale's passing. She'd been meaning to send this gift to us for a while but had never gotten around to it. I opened the box and gasped. Inside was a large needlepoint sampler of Jeremiah 29:11.

No one—not even Margie—knows about my life verse. There are more than fifty thousand verses in the Bible, and Mildred could've chosen any one of them to send, but she chose "mine." I cried. A lot. It felt like a little message from God that He actually saw me. He knew my sadness and—still—He had plans to give me hope and a future.

Margie asked me one day if I was angry with God over Dale's death. Sad? Yes. Angry? No. It made me think, though. I've talked to many people who *are* angry with God over many things—not just the loss of their spouse. Books have been written about it. Sermons have been delivered. Debates have raged. So, what if you *are* one of the angry people? How do you deal with this crushing loss without letting your anger destroy your faith?

It's totally okay to be angry with God. He can take it. Even Jesus displayed anger toward God. His last words on earth were, "My God, my God, why have you forsaken me?" (Matthew 27:46). Anger is part of the human condition we all understand. And the loss of your spouse—or your child, your parent, your health, or your job—can send you down a long spiral from which it's hard to recover. So where do you go with that anger? How do you respond when your prayers are not answered? Do you back away from God? I hope not. God would be totally fine having the anger discussion with you.

People journal, pray, drink, use drugs, tune out their family and friends, or drop out from society, yet some are still really angry with God. If God is all powerful, then why would He allow this to happen to you, to your spouse, to your family? It's a fair question, but asking "Why *me*?" is also a selfish question. No one ever says, "Why *them*?" Faith is not based on what we get from "Santa Claus." If we only love God because of what we get from Him, it isn't really faith.

There is no guarantee in life that we will get everything we ask for, hope for, or pray for. Yet even strong Christians search Scripture to find that assurance. So, if Christians can't count on some type of break from God in the bad times, what's the point? My son, Beau, is an Old Testament scholar and a wise and kind man. When I posed this question to him, his response was:

Mystery is a part of everyday life. Humans are not and cannot be ultimately knowing of the good and bad things that happen. When we reflect on things that happened in the past, often they turned out differently than we first imagined. Bad things weren't as bad as first thought and some good things didn't end well. Humans lack divine perspective. Anger with God often happens when people don't understand the ultimate, divine purpose of events in human history. Though we search for divine purpose, we don't get a final, precise answer.

And though God will sometimes intervene with a miracle, God does not compromise free will. Some choices result in poor outcomes. If we want to have the opportunity to express free will, we also have to live with the results. Bad things do happen to good people and we feel like we don't deserve it. Just as often, we do things that deserve serious punishment, but God forgives us.

It was a simple and meaningful lesson. If you expect that all will go well every day, that you will never suffer heartache or illness, you are bound to be severely disappointed. Instead of asking God to conform to our wills, maybe the lesson is that *we* should change *our* outlook.

We can all look back on times we've fervently hoped and prayed for something to happen and things did not go the way we wanted. Years later, we look back with relief that it *didn't* go as we wished. Sometimes God has something better in store for us.

Even if God does move in great and miraculous ways, you may not see it if you're not looking. Is there a time in your past when you saw God's hand in your life? Do you have a journal describing a time when you felt blessed by God? Have you ever written your prayer requests in your Bible? If you can look back and know God was there for you in the past, it can help you to trust Him in your present circumstances and can direct your future. And the decisions you make now will dictate the memories you'll look back on tomorrow.

So how can you hope to remember the blessings of today when life seems so uncertain? If you haven't kept a journal before, now may be a good time to start. If you're not much of a writer, maybe a photo journal would be a better option. Or keep a small notebook in your car to write down little blessings as they happen. It's great to look back at those little notes on days you feel like God doesn't see you. Sometimes just telling someone that God has impacted you in some way makes Him seem more real and relevant in your life.

Sometimes there is a deeper lesson to learn and a higher purpose at work. My friend Mary Jane told me her husband Don's long illness allowed him to find his way to a faith walk with God—something that may have never happened without the terrible reality of his dying from cancer. She was so grateful Don lived long enough to have his spiritual awakening, and—even though Don did not survive—she is forever thankful to God for His wisdom and faithfulness.

I spoke with Susan, a military widow whose twenty-eight-year-old husband, Irv, was killed by a sniper while on patrol in Mosul, Iraq. Susan lived that awful moment military spouses dread when she opened the door to an Army chaplain who said, "On behalf of the United States Army, we regret to inform you . . ." Susan and Irv had been high school sweethearts; she was twenty-seven when Irv was killed in 2006, and they had two children who were then six and eight years old.

Susan was raised in the Catholic church and considers herself a Christian who trusts in God. But she experienced a crisis of faith when Irv died. She was very angry with a God who would allow Irv to be killed while serving his country, and she shared that it has taken nearly eight years to turn the corner on her anger.

Susan became extremely depressed over Irv's death. Finances were an issue. She had been part of a military family for years, and now she was going to have to move away from the base. We both cried when she talked about leaving the home she and Irv shared. She sat on the floor in Irv's closet and cried until her young daughter told her they needed to go. She shared that depression led her to make poor decisions during that time—including getting into an unhealthy new relationship.

I asked Susan what helped her move beyond her anger. Did she regret Irv serving in the military? She replied:

I *was* angry that Irv and I didn't get to live the life we planned. But my kids needed me. The kids suffer just as much as adults but don't have the emotional ability to deal with things. My son was depressed and my daughter—a true daddy's girl—held in all her emotions. Irv joined the military to give his kids a better life. We wanted to move away from New York City to raise the kids. We wanted them to be able to go to college—something we couldn't have done on our own. Now they can go. So while I'm so sorry Irv was killed, I don't regret he served. I decided to be grateful that Irv got to have children. I was grateful for the time we had together and that I had the love of a great man for thirteen years.

And her secret to moving forward? "Time. We always talk to God and we want things right now. But God's timing and ours don't always align."

My friend Lani is a commissioned pastor six months away

from ordination, and her husband, Tyler, is a lieutenant colonel in the US Army who has served multiple combat tours, including Iraq, Afghanistan, and Saudi Arabia. They serve with Military Home, a ministry developed by Mountain Park Community Church to serve the strong demographic of military families who attend. But because our church isn't near a military installation, they wrote their own material and developed a ministry program specific to the needs of our congregation.

Lani pointed out that in the military you always know your loved one could be killed, but you think it's going to happen to someone else and that *you* will get to support *them*. There is survivor's guilt in the military, which—along with honor, love, and respect—leads the military to take care of their own. Tyler and other active duty soldiers make a point of engaging with families of those killed in action. Soldiers name their new baby after a fallen comrade. Even kids rally around and walk beside the children of fallen soldiers.

Christian faith is prevalent in the military, and Lani's experience is that most people don't question God's role in the death of their spouse. However, if you do have anger about your situation, Lani suggests trying to articulate and objectify your anger. Write down your thoughts. What are you angry about? Who makes you angry? What—specifically—did they do to your spouse? She finds you get angry with God because you're unable to articulate the anger that comes from sadness, fear, and frustration. And sometimes there is no one to take responsibility—so you blame God.

Many people who lose a spouse to suicide blame God, their spouse, *and* themselves. They may face mixed emotions because their loved one is responsible for his death. So while survivors mourn their spouse's death, they may be angry with him too. They also tend to question their role in their spouse's decision and wonder if they could have affected the situation by doing something differently.[1] In her article "The Bible and Suicide," Mary Fairchild says, "No one can truly understand the depth of someone else's suffering or the reasons that could drive a soul to such desperation. Only God knows what is in a person's heart. Only He knows the extent of pain that might bring a person to the point of suicide."[2]

I asked Sandy's widower, Bob, how his faith held up over this difficult time. Both he and Sandy had been prominent, visible people at our church. Bob helped Sandy with her job when she became too ill to continue, and he took over Sandy's position as head of children's ministry after she died. He wanted to stay for the children's ministry kids who were grieving her loss. He couldn't have Sandy die and then "disappear from the kids' lives too."

Regarding his faith walk, Bob is "still in the process of redefining where [he lands] on a few things." He suggests that at some point "you have to heal yourself. You can choose not to take other people into your sadness with you." Bob has also learned more about boundaries. He no longer takes on other people's baggage. "I'm a work in progress. God's not done with me yet." I had to smile when he said it. Dale said the same thing about once a week.

My friend and neighbor Penny lost her husband, Paul, in 2006 before we met. He died from a massive coronary at age fifty-three while singing in the choir at a church service just before Easter. She said, "Everything about my life changed in less than ten minutes. I was almost forty-nine years old and a widow. It would be weeks before I even began to understand what that would mean for me, for my life."

For a while, Penny just lived the days, meeting her obligations, surviving. She read books on death and dying and grief. She was on a constant search for the answer to "Why?" even though intellectually she knew there wasn't anything beyond the physical limitations of the body to explain Paul's death. She didn't turn away from God, but their personal relationship became more distant. She no longer believed God would answer her prayers and—for a long period—she quit praying much at all. She was more "deeply sad than angry."

It took Penny more than six years, with the help of a wonderful spiritual counselor and the friends in her covenant group, to find her way back to a deeper faith in God. She became a student of the Bible, religious texts, and commentary from a mostly intellectual viewpoint, which seemed safer than actually engaging with God.

Penny's little message from God came when she was unpacking books after a move to Chicago. She found a small book that had belonged to Paul called *The Only Necessary Thing* in which Henri Nouwen writes about learning to pray as a necessary part of living. She found a copy of the hymn "Amazing Grace" on a sheet of paper tucked in the book, marking the chapter on "Death and Eternal Life." She felt it was a personal message from Paul—and God—that she would be okay if she could find a way to a deeper trust and faith than she had before. Somehow, Paul's death brought her closer to understanding life and the frailties in all of us.

There is an unknowingness of God that must remain to

maintain the essence of a higher power. God is unfinalizable. As much as we would like for God to conform to our plans, that isn't how it works. Even God acknowledges that: "'For my thoughts are not your thoughts, neither are your ways my ways,' declares the Lord. 'As the heavens are higher than the earth, so are my ways higher than your ways and my thoughts than your thoughts'" (Isaiah 55:8–9).

I recently finished a wonderful Bible study called *Children of the Day* by Beth Moore that sums up this concept far better than I could:

> Awake to our present season. Awake to our people. Awake even to our pain lest it end up meaning nothing. Awake to the clock ticking, conscious of the critical hour in which the soles of our shoes are glued to this globe. Awake and aware of what is to come, both the beautiful and the frightful.
>
> To be awake is to still have questions and not just tidy summations. Our Creator knows that once we figure anything out entirely, we sigh so deeply that our lungs fill with water and we sink to the bottom with boredom.
>
> To be awake is to still grapple with mystery.[3]

What a concept, to embrace the mystery in each season in life—even the difficult ones. What should we learn? Why should we be grateful? Where can we serve?

Instead of asking, where was God in this?—or what's the point of life without my spouse?—it may be time to choose joy over sorrow, peace over anxiety, gratitude over anger. *Choose* might seem like an odd word here, but the mind is an amazing thing. You make hundreds of choices every day—some insignificant, some life changing. And the person who benefits most from choosing to be joyful, grateful, and content is *you*.

My friend Penny wrote, *Death is not always a quiet departure at the end of a life well lived. Sometimes it is brutal and stark and shocking. At the end we are left with our memories, our faith in God, and holding our loved one in our hearts until we meet again.*

The short answer is that we won't know the answer to why bad things happen when they do until we, too, meet God face-to-face. Even though we think we'd like to have all the answers right now rather than fathom the mysteries of God, I'd much rather wait to hear it from Him. God's not done with you—or me.

 # Your Story

What is your personal relationship with God? How did you get there?

Describe a time in your past when you saw God's hand in your life.

How has your faith walk changed since your spouse died?

Are you angry with God? In what ways did He fail you? Have you told Him?

Have you spoken with someone about your feelings?

If you were angry with God, how long did it take before you "forgave" God? What made you forgive Him?

In what ways has your faith walk sustained you during this time of loss and transition?

7

Is My Spouse in Heaven?

If we're going to have a discussion about where God was when our spouses died, pretty soon we're going to get to the next question: What about heaven? We arrive at yet another topic about which hundreds of books have been written, sermons given, and arguments delivered.

My questions were fairly pedestrian: Is Dale in heaven? Can he see me? Is he dating? (I know that's weird, but I did wonder.) Will he be waiting for me when I get there? Who gets to go to heaven? When do they go there? What do they do when they get there? If there is heaven, must there also be hell?

Though there is surprisingly little in the Bible about heaven, most of us have many thoughts about what it will be like. Much of what we think about heaven probably comes more from literature like Dante's *Paradiso* or *The Space Trilogy* and *The Great Divorce* by C. S. Lewis than from the Bible.

Heaven has been defined as the sky or firmament, the divine Providence, or a place of great happiness or bliss. Most of us think of it as the dwelling place of God, angels, and souls granted salvation. From childhood, we've seen pictures of angels with wings, playing harps, sitting on clouds, watching the world go by. We think of Grandma being "up there" with our guardian angel, watching over us while we deal with life's trials and tribulations. We watch movies like *It's a Wonderful Life* every year at Christmas, and we're pretty sure that we'd much rather make it to heaven than the alternative—also described by Dante in his *Inferno*. The wonderful part about not knowing many details about heaven is that you can imagine all you want about what it will be like when you get there. The one thing I know for sure is that it will be even more amazing than our wildest dreams—a place of immeasurable awe that will dwarf what we know.

Even people I've known who don't have a faith walk or who don't believe in God want to go to heaven—probably because it's better than any possible alternative. After my dad died, my mom asked me if I *really* believed in heaven. Indeed, I do. But when I think about someone I've known and loved for twenty-five years and wonder what happened to his soul, it takes on another dimension entirely.

Knights' Roundtable spent two years studying in the book of Romans. Yeah—two years. Some weeks it was a struggle. But I took something away from Romans that stays with me to this day—the concept of hope. Hope in God. Hope for salvation. We literally spent one entire evening discussing the meaning of the word *hope*—my friend Gene driving home the point that today's definition of hope is very different from hope in God. Society seems to use *hope* interchangeably with *wish*: "I hope I pass my test," or "I hope we get to go."

Webster's Dictionary defines *hope* as "to long for with expectation of obtainment." So much better! Instead of wishing to go to heaven when you die, it's ever so much better to "long to go there with the expectation" of it actually happening. This is the kind of hope that gets you through a time of loss and transition so you don't make seriously harmful decisions, the kind of hope that sees you through a bad report from the doctor, the kind of hope you need to parent children struggling with life.

According to the Christian faith, heaven will be home to all people who believe that Jesus is the Son of God who died for our sins and who rose again from the dead. By that measure, Dale is most certainly in heaven, and I'm so very grateful to have that assurance.

My friend Penny expressed the same thoughts about her late husband:

Paul was a deeply spiritual man. He read his Bible every morning. He lived a life of service and kindness. I knew, at a deeply profound level, that the God Paul believed in would hold him close and keep him safe and joyful. I never once worried about "where he went," and I find comfort in that still. I found it difficult to be angry at God when I held so tightly to the belief that Paul was there at His side.

When I asked Pastor Allan what he tells people who ask what happens to their loved one after death, he said, "The short answer is no one really knows." Even theologians disagree about *when* we go to heaven—as soon as a person dies or after a period of "sleep" when we're all gathered up in the clouds together. The only thing we know for certain is that after we die, our eternity is at the mercy of God.

So often since starting this journey I've wondered, *What would I have done if Dale hadn't known Jesus?* The truth is, I'm not sure. But I do know God extends grace—divine love, protection, and forgiveness—freely upon humankind. It's unearned and unmerited. You can't do enough "good works" to buy your way into heaven. Christians believe God grants us salvation through belief in Jesus *in spite of* our behavior. None of us deserves to go to heaven, but through God's mercy and Jesus' death, we get there.

If you've lost your spouse to suicide, you may have wondered, *If a Christian commits suicide, can he still go to heaven?* Many religions believe suicide is a sin and some refuse certain sacraments to those who've killed themselves. Some Jewish cemeteries bury people who commit suicide in a separate part of the cemetery. Some Catholic cemeteries will not permit interment. If you've experienced this while dealing with your grief, you have my sincerest sympathies. It must make an unbearable situation immeasurably more difficult.

Salvation is the state of being saved from God's judgment, and many scholars believe suicide is a sin that can be forgiven. The Bible tells us at the moment of salvation a believer's sins are forgiven. All of our sins, even those committed *after* salvation, are no longer held against us. So, we're saved by God's grace, not by our own good deeds. In the same way that our own good works don't save us, our bad ones cannot keep us from salvation.[1]

Though this is a simplistic answer to a complex question, I hope it will lead to further discussion with your minister, spiritual advisor, therapist, friends, or support group. While many support groups are available (both in person and online) for survivors of loved ones who committed suicide, some survivors are too grief stricken or feel too embarrassed or guilty to share their grief with others. Some survivors don't want people to know the cause of their loved one's death. They encounter people who simply don't know what to say, so they say nothing and step away from the relationship.

I asked a minister friend, Kevin, what he would say to someone who questioned their spouse's salvation. What about good people who don't have a faith walk? What about bad people? What about people from different faiths? His answer was very simple: "I'm going to leave those decisions to a great and merciful God." It's one of those mysteries that we won't know until we see God, and I'm adding it to my list of questions to ask when I get the opportunity.

The better question is, what can I do to assure my own salvation while I'm still here to do something about it?

If you have no faith walk, it's not too late. But where do you start? Many ministers suggest you begin by reading one of the Gospels, the first four books in the New Testament. Consider starting with Mark, which is short and story driven. Follow up with Matthew, which was written to a Jewish audience, paints "the big picture," and has lots of quotations from the Old Testament. It's an excellent starting point for people of Jewish or Muslim roots. Luke, written by a doctor, is more analytical and detailed. John is poetic, with more commentary and theology; you may want to read that after you get the story down. So, if you'd like to learn more about Jesus and His teachings, do start in the Gospels. Then move on to the book of Acts, which details the days after Jesus' death and the beginnings of the church.

Many of the people who provide testimony about Christianity and Jesus in the Gospels and in Acts were persecuted and died for their faith in Jesus. Eleven of Jesus' twelve apostles (including Matthias, chosen to replace Judas Iscariot, who hanged himself) were martyred by some extraordinarily cruel methods on the "basis of two things: the resurrection of Christ and their belief in Him as the Son of God."[2] While that may seem a depressing place to start, for me it was very faith affirming. Those early disciples actually made the supreme sacrifice to spread the good news of Jesus' life, death, and resurrection. Do you think you could find eleven people who would lay down their lives for something they didn't fervently believe? Me neither.

If reading the Bible seems to be too heavy or too frightening a place to start, consider reaching out to a Christian friend. What's their story? Ask how they came to believe in God. Ask if they *really* believe this stuff. It may not convince you, but it will definitely lead to a most interesting conversation!

If you don't have a Christian friend, try a local church. Go more than once. Ask for a Bible—most churches will give one to you. Ask about grief counseling. Check into their support groups. Get involved. Although getting involved in a church isn't the only way to begin and build a relationship with God, it's an invaluable spiritual resource—and offers an opportunity to connect with others on a deeper level. However, finding the right church for you can be like finding the right spouse. You have to be willing to "kiss a few toads" to connect with the Prince of Peace.

Your Story

What do you think heaven will be like? Where do your ideas come from?

Explain how your thoughts about getting into heaven fit in with your faith walk?

Have you changed how you think about death and heaven now that your loved one has died?

How do your thoughts about heaven impact your relationships going forward?

8

Who Am I Now?

So, who am I now? Who am I *really*? It's a question nearly everyone grapples with at some point in life—when you retire, after you graduate, after a major success or failure, after the death of someone important to you. Nearly all of our lives, we are defined by our relationship to someone else—we are someone's daughter, sister, wife, mom, widow. You probably have friends you describe that way—your minister's wife, your friend's daughter, your boss' spouse. It's a way of connecting the dots of your relationships.

For years, many of my acquaintances knew me primarily as Erin and Beau's mom. I still cherish that role and—if I need to have a label—that's one I choose. But my children are adults living their own lives, and my day-to-day, hour-by-hour mothering chores have greatly diminished.

When my children left for college, I moved into my "Dale's wife and administrative assistant" years. I spent hours a day talking on the phone with Dale's clients, who knew me first as his "scheduler" and were later surprised to know me as his spouse.

Dale told me nearly every day that he couldn't do it without me. I felt needed and fulfilled. When Dale died, I not only lost my husband, but I also lost my career identity. I felt like "a (wo)man without a country."

Are you there, too? While you may still be someone's child, a mom, *and* a widow, you may be struggling with who you *really are* without those labels. Did life as you knew it cease to exist when your spouse died? Did it feel like you became a completely different and invisible person? For me, the process continues.

After Dale died, I made a conscious decision to become "the perfect widow." When I look back to that decision, I think, *Why would I choose* that *label as how I'd like for people to see me?* But choose I did. I wanted to honor my marriage and to have people think I could handle Dale's death in a God- and husband-honoring fashion.

As I mentioned earlier, Dale and I were very active at our church, and we knew a lot of people. On the day following Dale's funeral, Erin sang at each service at Mountain Park. Allan spoke about Dale's death each time he introduced Erin. I was there for the third service, and there was an audible gasp. Dale had died during spring break week, and a number of people had just returned from vacation the night before. They hadn't yet heard.

I left just before the service ended because I didn't think I could handle the benevolence that would follow. I am a crier of the highest order and—for sure—I would lose it.

When I returned to women's Bible study a couple of weeks later to share Dale's story, there was an outpouring of love unequaled in my experience. We hugged. We cried. We hugged some more. They prayed for me, provided meals, sent cards. One friend sent a card every week for a year. People I didn't know well called to check on me.

One of my strongest memories of that time was also the most interesting. A woman attending my Bible study pulled me aside after class one day.

"I wanted to tell you that I've been watching you."

My first thought was, *Huh? Watching me?*

"I wanted to see how you would handle all of this. You always seem so upbeat and positive; I wanted to see how you would handle the loss of your husband. Are you still optimistic now?"

My second thought was, *Well, that's honest.*

She went on to say she was impressed and surprised with my composure and I must really believe all of this "God stuff."

The "perfect widow persona" must have been working—to the outside observer. On the inside? Not so much. What about you? Perfect widow? Total wreck? Somewhere in between?

With Dale's death, I lost two of my main "identifiers": Dale's wife and Dale's administrative assistant. The vast majority of my time for the past twenty years had been spent filling those two roles. Most of the rest of it was spent serving at church—where I was wearing my "perfect widow" mask. So when someone I knew only casually admitted she'd been watching me, I doubled down on my mask. It kept me busy for most of the first year of widowhood.

My friend Penny was worried about her mom when her dad died after a short battle with lung cancer. Penny and her sister stayed after her dad's funeral to help Lucy clean out closets, get her paperwork in order, and handle her finances. They stayed busy getting her settled into her new life, but Penny was impatient with the way Lucy was handling widowhood. Lucy wasn't getting out enough. She ate popcorn for dinner. She was only sixty-three and was acting like the best years of her life were behind her.

Penny didn't realize then that you never really "settle" into anything. She didn't know until her own husband, Paul, died six years later.

I didn't get it when my dad died, either. I hate to tell you, but the truth is my emotions didn't catch up with me until year two of widowhood. After I'd taken charge of my financial universe, written all of the thank-you notes, and marked all of life's annual events, I hit the "What now?" wall. I was fifty-seven years old, and I wasn't sure what I wanted to be when I grew up. I wasn't working, my kids were grown, our big transition at church was complete, and—for the first time in my life—I questioned my identity.

In his book *Transitions, Making Sense of Life's Changes*, William Bridges discusses "the difficult process of letting go of an old situation, of suffering through the confusing nowhere of in-betweenness, and of launching forth again in a new situation."[1] I could totally relate to the "confusing nowhere of in-betweenness," but I was far from embracing my new situation.

It's one thing to *know* that you've lost your spouse, but it's an entirely different psychological process to reorient and redefine yourself after that devastating event. You know you "have crossed some kind of threshold and there's no going back. [Your] old life is gone," but you haven't yet encountered anything that feels like a new beginning.[2]

But I knew I didn't want to be the perfect widow forever. You too? It's exhausting. And—more importantly—it has nothing to do with the truth.

Dale and I had an intense marital relationship. He would've told you that I was the best thing that ever happened to him. I greatly admired his wit, his intellect, his devotion to our family, his intense desire to do everything well. He brought strength to our home. I brought joy to his universe—most days. After Dale's death, one of his coworkers sent a note that read, *I can count on one hand the number of wholesalers' wives who were a bigger part of their spouse's business than you were with Dale.*

When Dale was alive, I felt the magnitude of our relationship every day—even when he was traveling. Some days it was so intense it was overpowering. Now, the space inside me previously occupied by that passionate relationship was strangely empty. I went from having someone think I was the most amazing person on earth to feeling invisible and vacant. We have to be careful when we're empty inside. If we're not, we can make awful choices regarding what to pour into the void—drugs, alcohol, sex, people who don't have our best interests in mind.

My wise friend Osa, who was recovering from a divorce, once told me, "Kim, we are mourning something we never really had." It was a profound statement that I continue to ponder. It's an idealized relationship we are grieving and—in some ways—it's easier to cherish someone who is no longer alive. When you look back toward your marriage, you may find you remember the good things much more than the bad, and—in your memories—you don't have to deal with the complexities of a real live husband.

There were days during my marriage when I would have happily left, never to return. But I loved Dale, loved being married, loved the partnership, loved the working relationship, and loved the daily struggle to find a way to be a couple.

So who are you without your spouse? Do you tend to identify yourself by what you *do*—volunteer at church, play games, travel, cook, ski, needlepoint, read? Or are you able to determine who you *are*? Even when I looked at my roles in life—daughter, wife, mother, friend, teacher—I still defined myself by what I did. And in scheduling my days, I tried to fill the hole with more things to do. I signed up for classes, traveled, renovated my home, entertained, went out with friends, and continued to volunteer at Mountain Park. It's not all bad to fill your days (more about this later). However, if you're struggling with your identity, these may be avoidance tactics.

Ultimately, all of those roles and activities will fall away and you will remain. If you never have another romantic relationship, accept another job, take another trip, or find another hobby, then how do you define yourself?

We are taught from a young age to be humble and not to be self-centered. If we learn to follow those instructions, we can sometimes veer far away from having to be introspective about what we feel inside. People have spent millions of dollars and thousands of hours in therapy trying to discover the meaning of life and how they fit into it. Authors have made a fortune trying to help us figure out our purpose in life and giving instructions on how to achieve our goals.

Maybe you can try to think about yourself in terms of how other people describe you to see if you could find some truth there. I literally wrote a list: happy, nice, fun, funny, quick witted, smart, loyal, honest, opinionated, emotional, stubborn, devoutly

Christian. It was the "Girl Scout" version of me, but it was a place to start. We *are* all of those things, and—somehow—the sum of all those descriptions, all the life roles, all the labels, and all the things have met up with your soul to become you.

While there may be many things you should and will change and improve, it's okay to begin right where you are. But can you come to terms with being a widow without truly embracing that label?

My eighty-four-year-old widowed mother has many widowed friends. Many of them were married for more than fifty years and are not planning to move on to another romantic relationship. In my mom's case, she was married to her "dream man" for nearly sixty years, and she's certainly not going to move on to someone less dreamy now. Unless something unforeseen happens, she'll remain a widow. But she has most definitely not embraced the label.

Mom called me one day upset that a friend had invited her to go to lunch with "the rest of us widows," saying, "We have to stick together." Mom was boiling mad and refused to go.

"Mom," I replied, "she didn't mean anything by it. She was just asking you to go to lunch."

"I don't care! I don't even like to say the word *widow*. I am not going to be defined like that."

I laughed out loud. That made her madder. But I completely understand the sentiment. I felt the same thing at a widow's support group I attended—once.

A new Bible study friend who was widowed invited me to join her at another church for a widow's support group that met on the first Saturday of each month. She wanted to attend and didn't want to go alone. As much as I am a joiner and a doer, surprisingly, I'm not much of a support grouper. I absolutely acknowledge the need for support and sincerely appreciate the Herculean efforts made by many people who facilitate these groups. A number of widows shared that their group made all the difference for them. I just hadn't gone. But I really liked my new friend and, if she didn't want to go alone, I was in.

We drove up and found the group on a huge church campus. About sixty women were in attendance. They had great food, a speaker, and table favors, and the women were very social. They had plans to go to movies, to the theater, walking on Saturdays, church on Sundays, meetings once each month.

At some point in the meeting, we all went around the table and told our stories. That's when I knew I wouldn't come back. Some of the widows were "new," some were very angry, some were resigned to widowhood, and some had been widows for more than twenty years. *Twenty years.* It appeared they *had* accepted the label. All I could think was I didn't want to be sitting there telling my story twenty years from now. If I remain Dale's widow until the end of my days, so be it. But I'm not going to put that at the top of my "who I am" list. Maybe I *am* my mother's daughter after all.

Whether you choose to embrace your new normal or whether you fight it, you will, indeed, *live* a new normal. Other people—even those people who love and support you—see you in a different light. *You* probably see yourself in a different light. So, how do you redefine yourself?

It's hard to explain if you haven't lived it, but I'm trying to live each day as completely "in the moment" as I can. Sometimes when you're dealing with the day-to-day struggles of life, it's easy to take things for granted—the darling kids, the loving husband, the roof over your head, the fact that you could just get out of bed and do it again today. I had hundreds of those days too—until Dale died.

Suddenly faced with the reality that I would never again get to be annoyed by the things he did that drove me crazy, that I wouldn't have to run another list of mailing labels at midnight, that I wouldn't have to make a hundred business-related phone calls in a day, that I would never again get to ask his opinion or tell him I loved him, I embarked on a quick learning curve about what is *truly* important. I won't get a do-over with Dale, but I will not make that mistake going forward.

If I could have one positive thing come from Dale's death, it would be the ability to explain *in words* the utter, overwhelming sadness of the loss. One of the primary differences between the death of your spouse and the loss of anyone else is that you have a level of physical intimacy with your spouse that you just don't have with other people. That combined with the sheer amount of time you spent together heightens the loss. Until you live it, I'm not sure you can totally wrap your thoughts around the crushing magnitude of losing a beloved spouse.

Even as a strong woman with a powerful faith walk, a wonderful family, and a large support group, I was brought to my knees by Dale's death. I've totally changed how I think about life, marriage, and myself. Whatever happens in my future, I will never be the same.

After I shared my story with the women's Bible study at Mountain Park, my dear friend Chris sent me an e-mail that read in part, *Thank you so much for telling your story today. It will make a difference in so many lives. And I know who you are—a beloved child of God.*

That's a label I embrace.

Your Story

How have you changed the way you think about yourself since your spouse died?

Explain how other people treat you differently since your spouse died.

What life events keep you so busy that you don't have time to think? Is that a different kind of avoidance tactic?

Which "life labels" did you lose in addition to "spouse"?

What efforts have you made to embrace your "new normal"? How's it going?

In what ways have you successfully redefined yourself?

9

Does Life Continue in Your Husband's Home?

As you settle into your "new normal," have you started to make peace with living alone in the home you once shared with your spouse? Have you made some changes, or have you decided to leave everything the way it was when he lived there?

I absolutely loved our house—it was going to be our "forever home." We were going to work another five years and retire to live the good life surrounded by our fabulous neighbors. We made lots of plans for "when we had time," but that time never came.

The first thing I did was move into Dale's office. I'd always occupied a small roll-top desk off to one side while he sat behind his huge executive desk in his huge leather chair. One day when I was working while facing the wall at my smaller desk, it occurred to me that I could sit at the big desk. Dale's desk. I could look out the window instead of facing the wall.

Dale had worked from home throughout his career—normal for wholesalers who called on clients at their offices. We'd spent hundreds of hours in that room. Now it was my office. I started with the file cabinets and shredded the client correspondence. I made my way to our storage closet and took stock of the lifetime supply of red Sharpies (Dale's writing tool of choice), highlighters (for when the Sharpie wasn't enough), Post-it notes, yellow legal pads, business trinkets, sales cases, and stationery. I found that I couldn't really throw away anything.

This was Dale's stuff. Dale's office. Dale's home. Dale's pool. Dale's street. Dale's friends. Dale's church. Everywhere I looked, everything I touched, everywhere I sat reminded me of Dale.

We'd had a huge fight while choosing that striped chair after church one day. He'd panicked when we purchased that new dining room set. He'd worked all day to hang the wrought iron panels in the dining room. We had watched TV and napped on that couch. We'd had dozens of guests in the living room. We'd hosted Knights' Roundtable at that table for seven years. A wonderful home filled with memories of the most interesting man in the world—who was dead. My home became a place of sad reminders.

Oh, I still entertained, Knights' Roundtable still met there, my Chick Flicks still came over to watch movies, and the fabulous neighbors were still there. I spent six months renovating my master bath to *House Beautiful* perfection. But I could not fill the space vacated by Dale.

Going to bed at night became a dreaded ritual. It's funny, because Dale and I often slept in separate bedrooms. He snored like a freight train, and I'm an insomniac. He retreated to the guest room so I could get some sleep—but I knew he was over there (and I could still hear him snoring). Always a night owl, I now found myself staying up later and later so I was completely exhausted when my head hit the pillow.

Does this sound familiar? Are you reading this at 2 a.m., postponing going to bed?

I started to think I would move. But where would I go? I still had my little dog, Weston, and this was his home too. It seemed to me that he waited every evening for Dale to come home. If we moved, Weston might worry that Dale couldn't find us when he returned. I know how crazy that sounds, but I couldn't move my dog. Maybe you can't move your dog either. Perhaps your kids want to stay. Maybe *you* want to stay so something feels . . . normal.

But I thought about moving. *Should I move back to Denver? Should I move up to Scottsdale? My brother lives in St. Louis. Could I live there? My mom still lives in my hometown. Maybe I should go "home." Someplace new?* I thought about it. A lot.

About a year after Dale died, I planned to spend a week in Southern California with Erin and Beau, who both lived in that area. I looked online for a condo that would accept a dog—to no avail. All of the places that would take dogs weren't quite what I was looking for, and the places I liked wouldn't take dogs.

Then—without warning—it didn't matter.

One day Weston had a small dot of fluid on his back between his shoulder blades. It looked like water and I thought nothing of it. The next day, the dot was bigger. The day after that, the dot was the size of a half dollar and did not look good. I called the vet.

Weston had a skin infection. We tried antibiotics and ointments, but nothing helped. Over the weekend, Weston became extremely lethargic. He'd been diabetic for years and required two insulin shots every day after food. He stopped eating, so

I couldn't administer his insulin. I bought baby food, made chicken, and offered his favorite string cheese. Nothing worked. We'd have to go back to the vet on Monday.

Sunday night about midnight in a driving rainstorm, I took Weston to the emergency vet. I didn't think he'd live until morning. They did emergency surgery to remove the infected area. Thirty-nine staples held Weston together.

For humans and for dogs, a normal fasting blood sugar level is between 70 and 99 mg. Weston's blood sugar level soared to 770 mg. I spent one month and thousands of dollars trying to get his blood sugar under control—without success. At the end of July, after one final excruciating night at home with my dying dog, I had Weston put to sleep.

I stood in my vet's office and sobbed. A year after my husband died, a year of being the perfect widow, a year of running all of my teams at church, a year of teaching Bible study, of being a mom, a daughter, a friend—the final, crushing blow was the death of my fifteen-year-old twenty-pound West Highland Terrier.

Have you "hit the wall"? Was it the death of your beloved pet? Maybe your roof leaked or your dishwasher died. Maybe it was watching a *Mad Men* marathon at two in the morning when you ran head-on into "new normal" and knew something needed to change.

I called Christine to see if I could come over. She met me with a cocktail and a hug. We floated in the pool and cried. We discussed dogs, husbands, life, friendship. We cried some more. After a while I went home to my empty house and cried.

The next day, I received an e-mail from the owner of one

of the vacation rentals that didn't accept dogs. They had a cancellation. Did I still want to come? Erin had gone on a trip to Amsterdam, so I called Beau to see if he wanted to meet me in Laguna Beach for a few days. I rented the condo, stopped my mail, and drove 400 miles from Phoenix to Laguna to meet Beau.

When we walked into the condo, we stopped in our tracks. The condo, which had looked great online, was absolutely spectacular in person! Beau and I looked at each other and laughed out loud. We dropped our bags of groceries and took pictures of every room before we invaded the gorgeous space. Friends who came to visit squealed with delight when we opened the door. Later I learned the owner also owns a fabulous home store in Laguna. No wonder!

Beau and I spent the week doing fun stuff—we took the ferry to Catalina, did the mission tour in San Juan Capistrano, had dinner and drinks in Laguna, and visited the Getty Villa in Malibu. It was the perfect antidote to the sadness of the weekend before.

On the last night of our stay, I said to Beau, "This place is so gorgeous, I'm going to buy it!"

Beau looked me straight in the eye and said, "You know, Mom, you *could* buy a place here."

And—just like that—an idea was born. I wasn't at all sure if I could afford Southern California, so we went online to look at properties for sale. We surfed for a while and finally entered my e-mail address into a real estate website so we could look at pictures. If I sold my home in Phoenix, I might actually be able to buy something here.

Beau and I went to dinner, and when we returned I had a voice mail from a real estate agent named Diana.

"Hi! How much longer will you be in town?"

"I'm leaving tomorrow."

"Flying or driving?"

"Driving."

"Wanna look at some properties before you go?"

"Yep."

"I'll meet you at 9 a.m. at Starbucks! Woo-hoo!"

With that, I started my home search. The next morning, Diana showed us five properties that were all terrific. We made plans to look again the next weekend.

Beau left and I drove back to Phoenix. *Phoenix.* How could I leave the place? Phoenix had been such a great fit for Dale and me. We had looked at seventy houses during our home search there and had settled on ours for its perfect floor plan, great golf course views, and its proximity to the airport and to Tucson, where Dale worked once a week. And our house happened to be on that perfect street with those perfect neighbors. How could I leave? How could I replace Mountain Park? How could I resign from the board? How could I tell Christine?

I barely remember the drive home. I was both excited and terrified—fear of the sadness I felt living life without Dale versus fear of the complete unknown. The one thing I do remember about that drive occurred just as I crossed the border from California into Arizona. I was out in the middle of the desert with a totally clear sky. I looked up and saw a huge, blinding rainbow. Literally, I could see every color through to violet. It was spectacular! At that moment, "Somewhere," one of two songs from my wedding to Dale, played on the radio. It was like God—and Dale—sending a message that it would all be okay.

I told my mom first. I worried she'd be sad I wasn't going to move to Chester, my hometown, but she thought Southern California would be perfect. "And if it doesn't work out," she said, "go someplace else." If she was ever disappointed I didn't move "home," she never said, and I'm eternally grateful.

Next I called my brother, who said, "We thought you might consider moving to St. Louis."

"I did, Brad. But the only people I know there are you and Lynn. There's really nothing there for me either."

Ultimately, Brad gave me his blessing.

I made four more trips to Laguna Beach and Dana Point, the next town down the coast, and finally made an offer on a condo with an amazing view. After a little wrangling, the offer was accepted. I owned a home in Dana Point, California—and in Phoenix.

I called my real estate agent friend, Osa, and we put together a plan to sell my home in Phoenix. I staged my home, put it on the market, and waited twenty anxious days before I received a nearly full-price offer. Sold! My buyers were scheduled to be out of town and didn't want to close for six weeks. I used that time to have a garage sale, sell most of my furniture, and begin the monumental task of packing fifty-seven years of life into boxes. My life in my beautiful home on my amazing street with my fabulous neighbors ended.

On the last day of my life in Phoenix, Christine and I stood in her driveway and cried. We'd shared a lot of joys and sorrows over the years we occupied each end of our street. We'd discussed husbands and children, hopes and dreams, life and death. I was her fun, enthusiastic cheerleader. She was—and remains—my devoted friend.

In the six months after I moved to Dana Point, I transformed my condo into *my* home—not Dale's—on purpose. I kept some beloved objects that reminded me of excellent times gone by—Dale's books, family pictures, the duck call. But I needed to be able to come home and rest, and there I could.

But here's what I know: You can move, but you cannot leave your emotions behind. You can't outrun your feelings. They move with you. Wherever you go, *you're still there*. It isn't possible to have that intense relationship for more than twenty years and to honestly believe you can pack those memories into a box for safekeeping. As my friend Pat remarked, "Don't you wish there was an off switch for your emotions?" Some days, Pat, some days.

Many days, I am completely content with my new normal in Dana Point. I still hear from my friends in Phoenix, and I've had many friends and family come to visit. I've been to see my family and have traveled with friends. I've filled my days with activities and have embraced my new world, but deep in my soul is a yearning for that singular lost relationship.

So, maybe we can embrace the longing. Bring it to a new relationship. Decide to not spend the rest of our lives being sad about something over which we have no control. And the fact is that all of us will arrive here some day. Most of us will lose someone significant and irreplaceable in our lifetimes.

So, how do we honor that intense relationship and still move forward? It's a daily struggle, a process, and a goal. When I began to capture some of what it's like to reclaim a meaningful life after losing your spouse, I realized how singular all of our stories are. Some of us are women; some are men. Some are young; some are old. Some have financial difficulties; some do not. Some have young children and jobs; some are retired. Some had a great marriage they long for; some are relieved that it's over.

John F. Kennedy once said, "There are risks and costs to a program of action, but they are far less than the long-range risks and costs of comfortable *inaction*." Wise words. But though you must eventually move forward, please know that there isn't a right time frame or an instruction manual that fits every situation.

Though my friend Penny cleaned out her dad's closets immediately after his funeral, she didn't want to clean out her husband Paul's closet for years. And her mom never once told her she should. Within a few months of her dad's death, Penny's mom sold her home and moved into a condo. Penny kept the home she shared with Paul for another seven years before she could sell it. Penny learned from her mom's journey six years after it began—far from over for her mom, just beginning for Penny.

A new neighbor and friend told me, "When my husband died, I decided that I could sit at home and wallow in it, or I could do fun stuff. I chose fun stuff!" She moved from Texas to Dana Point to be near her children. I appreciate the no-nonsense Texan within, and I embrace her pioneer spirit. If we have to get out of bed every day, let's make sure that it's worth the effort!

 # Your Story

What influenced your decision to stay in the home you shared with your spouse or to move to a new home?

How did your friends and family feel about your move? How did their feeling influence your decision?

What has it been like to rebuild your life as a single person?

List five of the best things to come from your decision to move or not move. List the least fulfilling.

If you had it all to do over again, would you make the same decision?

10

Dating after Twenty-Five Years of Marriage . . . or Fifty

A little more than two years after Dale died, my good friend Lori asked me if I would ever date again. My first thought was: Dating. At. Age. Fifty-nine. Yikes!

I told Lori I hadn't met anyone I was interested in dating, but I wasn't against the idea. I love marriage, I love men, I love to do "guy" things, and I definitely missed being in a relationship. My list of requirements was pretty short: Christian, tall, and not an ax murderer.

Since my dad and Dale had died, my mom and I had spent hours discussing what we'd missed most. For my mom, the single hardest thing was not having anyone to talk with at the end of the day. Even though my mom is absolutely capable of running her business on her own, she still misses having the second opinion, the vote of confidence, the partner to share the successes and difficulties. I totally get it. There just isn't anyone else to fill that role—not my brother, not her secretary, not me.

I, too, miss the conversation, the sparring, the finishing

of each other's sentences. But for me, the most difficult thing has been the absence of our intense marital relationship. Dale thought of me as special, vital in his world, and "the best thing that ever happened to" him. We lived in a uniquely involved marriage, and then Dale died. The absence of that kind of love has left a gaping hole. Even the lack of physical affection as simple as hugging is a painful loss.

When you think about life since you lost your spouse, what do you miss the most? Is it something as basic as hugging or talking? Financial security? Having to move from your larger home into something more affordable? Needing someone to help with the kids? All of the above? A hundred other things?

Would we like to have that back? Absolutely! Do we have to date to meet someone to work our way back to that type of relationship? Yes. Do we have the slightest clue how to do that? Not so much. And if you haven't dated since the last century, things have changed. A lot.

But the main question is, do you feel *ready* to date? If so, what's the next step? Seriously, how do you begin to date again after a marriage of twenty years? Or fifty?

In this age of technology, you have *lots* of options to meet someone. Match, OurTime, ChristianMingle, PlentyOfFish, eHarmony, JDate, Zoosk, SingleParentMeet, uDate—you name it! You can surf potential dates for hours at home. You never have to leave the building to decide that you would or definitely would not meet that person for coffee. You can sit at home and face rejection from someone you've never even met. Golly. Maybe I'll just get another dog.

Many of us have single friends and relatives who've dated

online—some with success leading to a committed relationship and marriage, some who have sworn off dating altogether due to an unfortunate experience. Have you thought about online dating? Have you already tried it? While there are obvious issues with meeting and trying to get to know a "virtual person," it does greatly expand the number of people you are likely to encounter—especially if your kids are grown or you're no longer working.

For my mom, online dating is not going to happen since she can't remember the password to get on her computer! Perhaps you, too, would rather go through more traditional channels—meeting someone at church, playing golf, or volunteering for a favorite organization or political campaign. If you had a good friend who wanted to introduce you to someone they respected and admired, maybe you would consider meeting that person.

Another thing that would come into play for my mom in Chester and for me in Phoenix is who would be watching us date? Chester is a small town—population 8,500, half of whom are incarcerated at Menard Correctional Center! Excluding convicted felons, nearly everyone knows everyone else and pays attention to who is dating whom. If Mom showed up with a lunch date at one of Chester's few restaurants, the news might make the local newspaper! No kidding. To some extent, that's true in any community.

My first experience with people watching my potential dating activities was at church. My neighbor Bill had been attending Mountain Park's men's Bible study during the week even though he and Christine attended a nearby Catholic church. He enjoyed the men's group and wanted to learn more about Mountain Park and to hear Allan preach. Bill met me at the greeter station; we went into church and sat near the front.

Later that week, I was at Mountain Park when Allan called me aside.

"I saw you had a date in church on Sunday."

"A date?"

"A tall guy with white hair."

"Oh my gosh, Allan! That was the husband of my good friend."

He raised his eyebrows.

"They attend a Catholic church, and he was here checking out *you*, not me."

We had laughed and that was that. Until about a month later.

I had just finished a board meeting at Mountain Park and was walking to the parking lot when the board president, Jerry, remarked, "I saw you had a date this weekend."

"Where?"

"Mellow Mushroom."

Mellow Mushroom? Mellow Mushroom! "Was the guy tall and did he look young?"

"Well, he was tall."

"That was my *son*!"

"Oh. I was kind of excited that you might have met someone."

Golly! I hadn't even thought of dating and was still the source of much speculation among my peers. So what would it be like if I actually did meet and date someone in Phoenix? I think I'd share a little of my mom's apprehension. Would I be nervous when Dale's friends met him? Would I be embarrassed if it didn't work out? Maybe. And I wasn't sure I'd ever able to bring a date to "Dale's house." It would've felt like he was watching. I know that's wrong thinking—it's just me.

So, back to Lori and her question. The reason she was asking was she had someone in mind for me. She had been talking to Doug (her husband) one day and told him they should fix me up with their friend. "You'd be perfect together," she told me. "Doug said we are absolutely not getting into the matchmaking business. I was going to drop it, but literally one minute later, the phone rang and it was that friend. He said he wanted Doug and me to come visit him in California, and he wanted me to bring him a date! He wants to meet a tall Christian who plays golf. So, would you want to meet him?"

Well. Here was a dear friend who wanted to fix me up with a longtime friend who was tall, Christian, and not an ax murderer. I was intrigued. But here's the thing. The last time I dated, I was thirty-five years old and fabulous! Dating at fifty-nine is another thing entirely. What are the rules of engagement? Do we pretend we're not interested when we really are? Do you tell him you like him? Is there an expectation that sex will happen sooner rather than later because "we're all adults here"? I'm not sure I have the dating skill set. Do you?

I was with Lori and another friend when we were having this discussion, and both did their best to assure me I was still fabulous. It's still a daunting thing to consider, but I said, "Sure, I'd love to meet him. Here's my one condition. I don't want him to think you're introducing him to some young, thin babe. If he's okay with that, then you can give him my contact information."

Lori passed along my contact information to her friend.

A couple of days later, I received a one-word text from him: "Hello . . ."

I "hello'd" back, and—with that inauspicious beginning—we were off on a fun, spontaneous texting adventure. I was shocked how much I enjoyed texting with a man I didn't know existed until that week, that we had so much in common, and that, indeed, we might be perfect together. Texting soon led to nightly phone calls, and within a week, we were planning to meet.

Wow! A date. With a nice, Christian friend-of-a-friend who, in all likelihood, is not an ax murderer. I consulted my adult children, my mom, and our mutual friend, Lori, to see if they thought I should go. My kids had already checked him out on Facebook and decided he looked "normal and safe." The resounding, unanimous reply was "You should go!"

And, just like that, I was on my way to my first date with a new person in twenty-five years. Yikes!

The resulting date was wonderful and extraordinary. While I could have predicted I would (and did) have a great time, I was absolutely unprepared for the intense emotions I experienced. I'd thought I might feel guilty about dating—that somehow it wasn't honoring my great marriage by having a fabulous date with an amazing man.

But I didn't feel guilty. The emotion I experienced was deep longing—longing I didn't know was there, concealed by the perfect widow's mask, by filling every moment of every day with activities so I didn't have time to consider I might be missing something, by not daring to think a new romantic relationship could be in my future. I was stunned.

Here was a man who checked off my "tall, Christian, not-an-ax-murderer" boxes and brought his own list of attributes: funny, charming, attractive, well mannered, talkative, well dressed, intelligent, hardworking, and in touch with his emotions enough to know he was looking for a serious relationship. When Lori asked about the three days we spent together, I texted, "Wow! Best. First. Date. Ever."

And it never would have happened if I hadn't taken the risk that is relationship. But that's just the beginning of the story. . .

Your Story

What are your thoughts about dating since losing your spouse?

If you could design another serious relationship, what would it look like?

What reservations would you have about online dating sites?

Describe the dating advice, guidelines, and restrictions imposed by your friends and family.

If you've dated or are currently dating, how has the reality of your experience compared with your expectations?

11

Oh My Goodness!
I Met Someone New

If we were to gather stories from our single friends—both divorced and widowed—all of their dating experiences would likely be different. Sadly, there appears to be a lot of "baggage" that comes with dating after the loss of your spouse or the demise of your marriage: children who are concerned about their parents dating, health issues, differing financial situations, wondering how to handle the physical side of the relationship.

Women commonly mention that men have significantly more dating options than women, and that is quite probably true. According to the US Census Bureau, nearly 700,000 women lose their husbands each year and will be widows for an average of fourteen years.[1] AARP reports that in 1999, there were over four times as many widows (8.4 million) as widowers (1.9 million).[2] The US Census Bureau confirms that 32 percent of women aged fifty-five and older are widows, while 9 percent of men over fifty-five are widowers.[3] This is attributed in part to the longer average lifespan of women.

Men who are my contemporaries—currently in their late fifties and early sixties—can entertain the idea of dating much younger women, which greatly expands the number of potential dates from which to choose. Women my age tend to choose from men who are significantly older, and as mentioned above, there are just fewer men in that age group.

The University of California in San Diego conducted a study on widowhood and found that by twenty-five months after a spouse's death, 61 percent of men and 19 percent of women were either remarried or involved in a new romance.[4] Many articles suggest that men tend to remarry more quickly because women traditionally manage the social calendar and more duties on the home front, and men seek someone to fill in that gap. Women expressed more negative feelings about forming new romantic relationships than men. Younger age was a predictor of becoming involved in a new romance for women, and higher monthly income and level of education were predictors for men.

On a more personal note, one friend remarked on how difficult it is to date someone with whom you have no shared history and none of the traditional reasons to get married. Most of us are not looking to have more children, our finances are in better shape than when we were younger, and we've already established our households. It's an interesting dynamic that we're primarily looking for companionship. It seems like it should be easier—but it's not.

A seventy-five-year-old man once told me, "Honey, ya gotta be careful about dating. All guys my age are looking for a nurse with a purse." Golly. Spare me. Perhaps you, too, are hoping *not* to be a nurse with a purse.

Maybe you're like me—a "what-you-see-is-what-you-get"

person. Do you struggle with not saying every thought that comes into your head and with the "game playing" in the dating arena? If you enjoy spending time with someone, are you going to tell him? Is that too pushy? Does it take away the "thrill of the chase"? All of your friends and family will have advice on this topic. If you do figure out the rules to the dating game and successfully adopt that behavior, are you then creating a dating persona that doesn't really reflect who you *are*? If your date falls in love with that person, what chance does the "real you" have?

Do you have friends who thought they had the most amazing connection with a date and then never heard from the date again? Maybe *you've* already had that experience. It's a heartbreaking thing to deal with at a time when many widowed singles are already stressed out and fragile. To lose a loving marriage with somebody who actually got you and who knew your innermost thoughts to move on to this impersonal, often electronic and extremely visual dating arena can be depressing at best, gut wrenching at worst.

One of the biggest fears about reentering the dating world is facing rejection. And any time you seek relationship, you risk rejection. It seems like every week we learn about a friend or neighbor who is getting a divorce. We read about famous movie stars who have been rejected by their equally famous spouses. That rejection can cause us to make poor decisions, to retreat to the safety of our homes, to swear off new relationships forever.

When I told my widowed friend Anne I was in the first stages of a new dating relationship, she said, "Give it three months and call me back." Anne was widowed after just five weeks of marriage. Her late husband, Bob, had suffered a heart attack in their kitchen with Anne standing there. She provided CPR for fifteen minutes until the EMTs arrived, but Bob didn't survive.

Anne just started dating again at age fifty. She is a fit, smart, and engaging woman who's been invited on dates by men of all ages, sizes, and interests, but many did not bring much to the "party." Anne is a life coach, and many potential dates wanted her to "fix them." Yeah. Not a great start to becoming the leader of her household.

Like Dale, Bob was a man with a lot of expertise in the business world. He knew how to make Anne feel special and how to take charge in social situations. He convinced her to leave behind her single status after two years of dating. They had a wonderful and intense—if heartbreakingly short—marriage. Anne knows if she had that great relationship with Bob, it can happen again; but it's going to take a lot of effort and a little, or maybe a lot, of luck. She's also found it really hard to date without comparing each new suitor to Bob.

Anne describes herself as a "no drama" person who brings little baggage to the equation and who doesn't want to enter into a bad situation. And she's picky. As she pointed out: as the dating pool gets smaller and the baggage gets larger, the chance of meeting someone with whom you can think of spending your life gets exponentially smaller.

Anne recommends taking it slowly. Write down some key questions. What is important to you? What will you not tolerate? What are deal breakers? One of the first questions she asks is, "How is your relationship with your ex-wife?" She wants a man who knows about life, who can take charge in social situations, and he must like animals—her animals.

After my amazing date in Sacramento, I returned to real life in Dana Point with a *new* "new normal." I continued to grieve my husband's death while coming to grips with the fact that I could be seriously attracted to another man. I couldn't eat or sleep for a month after coming home. I lost thirty pounds—and I decided to embrace that happy side effect. I spent hours convincing myself that it was okay to like someone new, that Dale would want me to be happy.

My new friend continued to text and call for several weeks, but then the calls started coming further apart. He texted that he wanted a long-term relationship, but "building a relationship for me means closer space and time. We don't have that in our favor. Could we talk?" You can fill in "the rest of the story." I'm grateful he called to share his concerns, and we remain friends. Dr. Seuss once said, "Don't cry because it's over. Smile because it happened." So I'm working toward feeling really happy that we spent some great time together and that I learned I could have intense, romantic feelings for someone new. But if I'm fully honest, I'm not quite there yet.

My friend Victoria captured my emotions very well when she wrote:

Perhaps one reason you are so knocked sideways by this whole situation is that you "dared to dream." You spent time with him and all of a sudden you could picture a different future, one that included being loved, being someone another person "can't live without," having someone tell you how beautiful you are, not flying solo into old age. You regained a glimmer of what you originally thought your future would look like. I think we work very hard to squelch those longings for that future when we're left alone. But there is still that little fire of hope we try to keep contained in a dark corner, somewhere safe. Being with him stoked those embers.

So true that I cried when I read it. But this is what I know: we survived losing a spouse, and we will survive dating. Life does, indeed, go on. Some of these statistics and stories might make you nervous about dating again. But I've talked to many people who've had a wonderful dating experience and who have happily remarried after losing their spouse.

What if you *do* find someone to love and he loves you back? What then? How does the new person fit into your life? Who dictates what happens next? You? Your children? Your friends? What happens with your financial situation? Where will you live? What if everyone you know has the same reservations about your new love?

Daunting questions. Nearly every situation is unique, and nearly every friend, acquaintance, and relative—especially your children—will have an opinion.

Young children may have the most to gain, or lose, in a new relationship. They will have to live with your new spouse. Speaking as someone who divorced with young children, I can tell you it's not always easy. Dale didn't have children when we married, but he had lots of ideas about how to raise them. I can only imagine how complicated it gets when you blend two families with children. What if the kids don't get along? Whose house will you live in? Is another spouse involved in some way? Golly.

Adult children deal with many of the same concerns plus another set of issues. Older children are concerned about their parent being swindled by the new person, worried their parent might move on and give "dad's money" to the new guy, or maybe hoping to keep the family home but mom wants to sell and move to a condo in Florida. A very dear friend lived through the heartache of her mother's death and later watched her dad leave all of their marital assets to his new younger wife and her children. It made the death of her dad all the more distressing. One widower said his kids didn't care if he dated, but they didn't want him to date in their hometown. They didn't want to have to *see* him out with someone else.

The Schwab Center for Investment Research advises, "It's going to take a little more planning than perhaps you did the first time around."[5] No kidding! One of the first questions you should consider is if your finances should get married too. This should definitely involve a "yours, mine, and ours" discussion well before remarriage. Many financial advisors recommend keeping your finances separate for a few years until you see how things work out. Some experts even recommend moving into a new home so you are starting in neutral territory. It's kind of a sad—but realistic—place to start a marriage.

Especially in community property states, it's extremely difficult to separate your finances from those of your significant other once they have been transferred into the same "pot." Older newlyweds also need to consider how remarriage might affect Social Security benefits, Medicaid/Medicare expenses, and 401(k) plans; who makes "end of life" and other medical decisions; and what happens to your estate when you pass away. Some financial experts advise against remarrying at all simply to avoid all of the financial complications.

Whew! Just when you thought finding the right person was the hard part! A family meeting and a trip to see a financial planner are definitely in order.

And what if your friends and family don't like your new love? Should they get to weigh in? The people pleaser within me wants all of my friends and family to be happy with me and the choices I make—dates and husbands included. However, this mind-set can eliminate the possibility of ever finding the one person on whom everyone can agree.

My friend Bob worked on Sundays, so he no longer regularly attended a church service after his wife died. He received much of his spiritual healing and enrichment through Christ-centered yoga offered at church. One of the teachers, Dawn, had gone through the demise of a difficult marriage; they found solace together and have since married.

Bob's younger daughter (and second child) asked, "How come I don't ever see you feeling sad about Mom? You have Dawn now, so you don't miss Mom." A heartbreaking and honest observation.

Bob had a great response. He told her it's like having your second child. "When you have your first child, you never think you can love a second child half as much. But the moment the second child arrives, you do. I didn't think I could love another woman like I loved your mom, but I do. God has given us endless capacity to love."

But what if everyone has the same objections about your new love? Should you be listening? Maybe. I returned to the wisdom of the web for some "red-light" signals and found a great article, "If He Does These 25 Things, You Need to Drop Him Like a Bad Habit." Awesome title. Great information.

The writer summed it up well when she wrote, "Chemistry, attraction, hope and passion can make the most logical ladies go a little loco. . . . You're a grown, intelligent woman; you know when someone is acting strange."[6] I read through her list of twenty-five red-light issues and found myself nodding along with her. Just to be clear, these character traits can apply to both men *and* women.

When you catch him in a lie, when he doesn't have friends of his own and doesn't want to meet yours, when his old girlfriends hate him and so do yours, when you realize you don't really know anything about him, or things just don't feel right, it's time to listen to your intuition. One friend who was lamenting the state of her second marriage knew all of these things about her husband when he was still her fiancé. I asked her why she married him. "It was easier than telling him I didn't want to get married." Wow. To avoid having a tough five-minute conversation, a dear friend spends the rest of her life in a bad marriage. Dale used to call this approach the "path of least resistance."

Maybe you've found the perfect life partner. Maybe you'd rather live life alone or with your amazing family and friends than find yourself in a bad situation. Time to take a step back and reevaluate. There are worse things than being alone, and as a wise friend recently pointed out, "we've already lived through worse."

 # Your Story

List the factors that would determine if you would consider getting married again.

What would your children think if you did? How much does that play into your decision?

Where would you live? What happens to your home when you die?

What arrangements have you made regarding your finances?

List any objections your family and friends have about your love interest.

List any concerns *you* have about your love interest.

12

Dealing with the Guilt of Surviving... And Being Happy Again

When the head of the cardiovascular ICU told me Dale's grim prognosis—paralysis, ventilator, silence—my first thought was, *Dale couldn't take it. He would go insane.* My second thought was, *I might too.* Oh, I rallied and made that deal with God that if Dale survived, I would be the most amazing caregiver of all time. I would make Dale proud. But I never got to find out if I could've held up my end of the bargain.

When I look back on that time, I feel guilty that I considered the best option for Dale might be for him not to survive—that there *are* worse fates than death. I've talked with many people who survived their spouse and who dealt with the guilt of surviving. As noted physicist Stephen Hawking once remarked, "The human capacity for guilt is such that people can always find ways to blame themselves." Brilliant and so true. Why is that? We didn't do anything to harm our spouses, but here we are wondering if it's okay for life to continue and for us to be happy.

One recently widowed friend in her seventies admitted that she thought she'd never date or marry again because she'd spent the past decade caring for her ailing husband. While she didn't regret that time, she wanted to spend her remaining years traveling and doing the things she and her husband hadn't been able to do due to his illness. She didn't want to take on another caregiver role. She felt guilty *and* selfish.

This appears to be especially common for survivors grieving spouses who had been ill over a long period of time. Knowing that a spouse is going to die takes a toll that is unimaginable. Trying to get through each day taking care of children, finances, medical issues, and just the everyday details of life while worrying about what's next is beyond devastating.

Many survivors I spoke with were mentally and emotionally exhausted from trying to shield other family members from much of the bad news. More than one person told me they started mourning their spouse and their marriage fairly soon after the initial diagnosis—the marriage relationship ceding ground to a caretaking arrangement. It's known as "anticipatory grief."

Anticipatory grief can carry many of the symptoms of regular grief—sadness, anger, isolation, forgetfulness, and depression. These complicated emotions are often coupled with the exhaustion that comes with being a caregiver. . . . In advance of a death we grieve the loss of a person's abilities and independence, their loss of cognition, a loss of hope, loss of future dreams, loss of stability and security, loss of their identity and our own.[1]

More than one spouse expressed relief when the suffering was over—only to feel more guilt for their thoughts. Gut wrenching. Two male friends confessed relief when each of their wives died following a battle with cancer. Their relief turned to guilt almost immediately—guilt that required therapy for each man and his children.

The teenage daughter of one friend wanted him to grieve her mother's death until *she* was ready to move on. That revelation made me think about something I've never considered before: though a family loses one family member, each person loses a different *relationship*. Losing a spouse is a completely different experience than losing a parent. The mourning process is so vastly different—the age of the mourners, the status of the relationship, the different levels of intimacy. It seems normal for a spouse to want to replace the intimate, intense spousal relationship sooner rather than later. But a child—unless extremely young at the time of the loss—will likely never replace a mother. To expect the grieving process to be similar is shortsighted and unrealistic.

If your spouse committed suicide, you may experience a different kind of guilt for not having been able to prevent such an outcome.

Survivors are often unaware of the many factors that contributed to the suicide and in retrospect see things they may have not been aware of before the event. Survivors will often replay events up to the last moments of their loved ones' lives, digging for clues and warnings that they blame themselves for not noticing or taking seriously enough. . . . If only they had done or said something differently, maybe the outcome would have been different.[2]

Suicide survivors often experience very complicated and prolonged challenges that lead to "higher incidences of rejection, shame, stigma, and the need to conceal the cause of death."[3] They feel an intense need to make sense of the death and why their loved one took his or her own life and to figure out what role—if any—they played in the events. Suicide survivors are at higher risk of suicide themselves, and their grief tends to last longer than that of other survivors.

While grief and guilt are normal responses to loss, sometimes normal support from friends, family, and clergy isn't sufficient for survivors of suicide loss. If you are dealing with suicide loss, please give yourself permission to grieve. But realize that you may need to seek professional therapy and/or attend special support groups for suicide survivors to develop healthy coping mechanisms, to set realistic expectations for your new life, and to find a way toward happiness going forward.

For the most part, I am a happy person—enthusiastic, optimistic, content, grateful. My kids, my mom, my family, and I are healthy. By far, the most devastating thing that's ever happened to me was the death of my husband. But I'm still happy. And I had happy moments fairly soon after Dale's death.

Stephen and Kris, longtime friends who drove down from Denver for Dale's funeral, stopped by the house before driving back to Colorado. We sat in the backyard and discussed the events of the week.

"How crazy is all of this!" they said. "Are you doing okay?"

Then, in mid conversation, Stephen asked about a large tiki head made from the bottom of a palm tree—the roots creating a crazy hairdo—planted in my yard.

"That's Rod Stewart," I said.

"Rod Stewart?"

I told them about spotting a selection of tiki heads for sale near the roadside in Wickenburg, Arizona, one Saturday when Dale and I were out for a drive. I had to have one! Three trips to Wickenburg later, I brought home my proud possession. It's a funny story involving a drunken tiki carver, rebar, and concrete. Upon observing the crazy tiki with the windblown hair, my dad christened him "Rod Stewart." In telling how Rod happened to be planted there, I got the giggles. Then we got into some serious laugh-until-you-cry laughing. It felt so good to laugh like that. And then I thought, *Wow. I shouldn't be laughing. It's wrong to laugh the day after my husband's funeral.*

I've had lots of happy moments since then, but for the first year following Dale's death, I judged myself for each one as I lived it. Have you done that? Is it okay for you to be happy and to enjoy life without your husband, or should you feel guilty? Do you wonder if he can see you being happy? What do other people think when you're happy?

These might be unusual questions, but many survivors feel guilty for a variety of reasons. Some spouses had an unresolved issue with their loved one and then she died. They weren't home when he had the heart attack. They had a fight the last time they spoke, and then he killed himself. How do you work through that? People also place a lot of importance on the "last moment" they spent with their loved one. It's vitally important to remember that your relationship is not defined by the last moment but rather by the whole picture.

If you look at the five stages of grief—denial, anger, bargaining, depression, and acceptance—guilt probably shows up in the bargaining phase—the "if only" phase. How often have you heard someone say, "If I had just stayed home from work that day . . ." "If I had only known that he didn't feel well . . ." "If only . . ."? Military widow Susan felt guilty over little things. "I started thinking if I hadn't argued with him, God wouldn't have taken him from me. If I had been nicer, he wouldn't have been killed."

In nearly every scenario, there is nothing that most of us could have done. We're *not* guilty of anything except being alive, yet we *feel* guilty.

If we had this conversation with anyone else, we'd have no trouble counseling them that it wasn't their fault, they couldn't have done anything more, and events were outside their control. And we'd *mean* it. But we don't believe it for ourselves. Because the death of anyone is nearly always out of our control, we often try to make sense out of something that our hearts and minds can't and don't want to accept or deal with.

My mom still goes over that last awful day of my dad's life. He suffered an intracranial hemorrhage at home while taking a nap, and his life was nearly over before Mom knew there was a problem. She still asks me if I think she could've done anything else for my dad. Should she have called an ambulance earlier? Do I blame her that he died? Absolutely not! But guilt still haunts her.

When Dale was in the cardiovascular ICU, a team of doctors had to convince me that he had no brain function, his condition was irreversible, and nothing could be done. This educated, experienced group of medical professionals couldn't fix Dale, but I felt guilty, as if somehow that would make it better.

Some people feel guilty for doing something wrong, for *not* doing something they should have, for *thinking about* doing something bad. Guilt over surviving your spouse is unlike any other type of guilt. It's not really "survivor's guilt," which comes after surviving an event in which many people perish, such as a plane crash. This guilt is similar to remorse felt by some people who think they didn't do enough to help someone. But surviving a spouse doesn't really fit there, either. Often the surviving spouse *has* done everything possible to care for her spouse, but he died anyway. If you want to categorize this guilt, file it under "false guilt." So how do you process guilt that isn't even real?

When someone we love dies, it's only human to try to find some type of rational explanation. And when the event is random—a stroke, an aneurysm, a heart attack, a prolonged illness—it's really difficult to find something or someone to take the blame. So we blame God or we look to ourselves. What could we have done better or differently? Often, the answer is *nothing*. "False guilt is a learned response triggered by something external to us—an outside demand we could not or did not meet. It's unreasonable, inappropriate, and unhealthy."[4] It's an effort to take charge of a situation over which we have no control.

The opposite of guilty is "innocent" or "blameless." If you really analyze the situation you're in, my guess is your actions in the passing of your loved one come much closer to innocent and blameless than they do to guilty, which, according to *Webster's Dictionary*, means "justly liable or deserving of a penalty," something for which you could stand trial.

Psychology Today cautions: "Your own [perceived] failure will not help bring someone back to life, nor will it make others who love you feel better about themselves. You need to gain your inspiration from the knowledge that your efforts are a tribute to [your deceased loved one]."[5] You'll probably never life a guilt-free life, but you can try to keep it manageable so you aren't limiting *your own* hopes and dreams in an attempt to pay tribute to your deceased spouse. Guilt in and of itself isn't a bad emotion, but it can consume you if you're not careful. "False guilt can result in depression and spiritual paralysis. [It] tends to be very 'me-centered.' The tendency is to think we'll never be good enough and to focus on our shortcomings."[6]

Most of the suggestions you'll find about dealing with guilt involve figuring out what you did wrong, apologizing to the offended person, and trying to make amends. But none of that applies here. One of the best suggestions I read is to *write down* what you perceive to be your responsibility. What, exactly, did you do wrong? Instead of rehashing the "if onlys," consider the reality of your situation. Once you acknowledge that—truly— you didn't do anything wrong, you may be able to turn the corner on guilt. If you can't get there on your own, talk with someone: a trusted friend, your minister, a therapist, or God.

Many years ago, after my first husband, Bud, and I divorced, I felt terribly guilty I wasn't able to save our marriage. I didn't want my children to be from a divorced home. *I* didn't want to be from a divorced home. Every night for years, I told God how sorry I was that we'd gotten divorced. Long after I married Dale, I still prayed that prayer. I could not release the feeling of guilt.

About five years after Bud and I divorced, a friend asked me to go to a Christian women's retreat. We were assigned to be group leaders and facilitated a small-group discussion on the events of the day in our room each evening. Somehow the topic of guilt came up, and I mentioned I still felt guilty over the demise of my marriage—some five years after the fact.

One wise woman said to me, "Have you asked God to forgive you?"

"Every day for the past five years."

"Kim, do you know what grace is? You were forgiven your divorce the first time you ever prayed that prayer."

I *do* know that. But somehow I thought if I remained guilty forever it would mean I was *really, truly* sorry. That's Kim Knight doctrine—not God's promise. To turn away from God's grace goes against everything I hold true as a Christian. You won't be surprised to learn I sobbed over that revelation and, right from that moment, I moved on.

So, you can spend hours researching grief, suffering, death, and guilt; or you can pray to God for relief, peace, and grace. I've done both, and I sincerely recommend talking with God. Once you give yourself permission to put away your guilt, you can start the healing process while still honoring your late spouse. My military friend Susan reminded me that you never really "move on." But you can *move forward* to enjoy whatever life has in front of you.

I've known and spoken to widows who never remarried, who

never had another romance. Some just never had the opportunity. Some were honoring their marriage relationship until they joined their spouse in heaven. Some admitted they perceived some reward to wearing that "perfect widow mask" forever—some special place in heaven for someone who never wavered in their love for their late spouse. I recently finished reading a novel in which a character remarked, "What kind of wife would I be if I left your father simply because he was dead?"[7] Perfect! Even the Bible espouses special treatment for widows and orphans. Truthfully, I get all of that. But if I never remarry, does that mean I loved Dale more than if I do find someone new? The thought has crossed my mind.

What about you? Have you thought about staying true to your late husband just to prove how much you loved him?

My mom and her peer group of widows are all in their eighties. She plans to live the rest of her life on her own—due in part to her small-town circumstances, due to her perception that my dad was a one-of-a-kind guy who will never be equaled, and due to some thought that she will honor her marriage and my dad to her dying day. There's a little bit of martyrdom going on there. But if you look up *martyr* in the dictionary, you'll find: "one who chooses to suffer death rather than renounce a religious principle; one who makes great sacrifices for a cause or principle; one who endures great suffering."[8]

Yeah. I'm not sure that's what I choose for me.

I absolutely loved and respected my husband. It was devastating to lose him suddenly at age fifty-six when we were getting ready to embark on the big adventure of owning our own business. But, honestly, there is absolutely nothing to be gained by choosing guilt, unhappiness, and martyrdom—which, if you look back to the definition, involves your *own* death. Even if there's not another romantic relationship on the horizon, embracing life and whatever it has to offer seems like a much-preferred way to honor my spouse.

My friend Penny looked back over the past nine-plus years and wondered what happened to the time she calls "the lost decade" of her life. After nine years, she finally understands her grief and its "ever-present place" in her life; "how moments of pure joy can coexist with a longing so deep it almost hurts, how you can love deeply and forever and still find room in your life and heart to live and love again."

There are no right answers to handling the death of a spouse, and all of our journeys are different. But the pain you have endured will equip you with greater empathy. Think what a powerful tool that could be in your life ahead! Instead of turning your sorrow inward in the form of guilt, channeling that emotion into your family, the people you know, the things you do, or the special person who may be in your future is a much more powerful tribute to your spouse.

Your Story

Which of your actions when your spouse died made you feel guilty?

If other people made you feel guilty, what form did that take?

How have you been able to make peace with your guilt and move forward?

If you were going to counsel someone else about this type of guilt, what would you say?

How do you apply that advice in your own life?

13

What Do I Want to Be When I Grow Up?

We meet new people almost every day. Each new relationship nearly always starts with two questions: What do you do? And, after a time, are you married? Such simple questions with such complicated answers.

The "What do you do?" question may be easy for you. You're a lawyer. You're a stay-at-home mom. You teach school. You work for an insurance company. You're retired. For all of our adult lives, we knew what we did. We knew who we were. We knew if we were married. We used to never even think about it when people asked. Now we do.

When people ask me what I do, I usually say, "I may be retired." They laugh, and we talk about what I *used* to do. But that generally leads to the fact that I worked for my husband for twenty years, which begs the question, "Are you married?" Whenever I say, "I'm a widow," the response is *always*, "I'm so sorry." What a sad place to begin. My widowed friend Mary Jane recommends, "Just say you're single." I've tried that a few times, and people always respond, "Divorced?" No . . . golly.

I did have one great response to my "I'm a widow" remark, though. I was in a store purchasing a new paper towel holder with a decorative finial that had to be removed in order to put on a new roll. The store owner told me that men didn't like to remove the finial; so if I had a husband, I shouldn't buy it. I said, "It's okay. I'm a widow," to which she replied, "Oh, that's fantastic!" She was mortified, but I laughed out loud! It felt normal and wonderful to have a happy memory attached to admitting I am, indeed, a widow.

When I first started thinking about moving to California, one of my primary reservations was that, if I move, no one there will know who Dale was. How ironic! While I needed to move away from Dale's house, Dale's street, and Dale's neighbors, I didn't want him to fade away to nothing. Now I meet people who don't even know *he* existed, and I struggle with the very basics of who *I* am.

When I started to tell people that I was working on a book, it felt kind of pretentious. Who writes a book about widowhood? I found myself saying, "I know that sounds depressing, but it's been really cathartic and uplifting." Really? Do I want to be someone who finds this uplifting? Yikes!

But you know what? It's been amazing to analyze how I actually *feel* about Dale's death. The wonderful people who have shared their stories have said the same thing. "I'm so glad I talked to you about this." "I've totally reexamined who I am." "I thought it would be sad, but it wasn't."

It's possible to bury your real emotions beneath a load of

activity. It's possible to sit at home and never move on from the life you knew and loved. It's possible to put your late husband on a "perfect late husband" pedestal and polish it while wearing your "perfect widow" crown until you, too, pass away. But having to figure this out in order to put my thoughts down on paper has been a tremendous opportunity for learning, for growth, and for *closure*. My hope is that this book offers the beginning of some closure to *you*.

So, do we want to close this chapter? Maybe. What stops us from saying a resounding yes? I'm not sure. It may have something to do with unresolved guilt about moving on. But this is what I do know: God willing, I may live for another thirty years, and I refuse to be confined to the "perfect widow" box. I want to live my life in a manner that says to my children, *I was not beaten by this. God showed me He has plans to give me hope and a future.*

So . . . what do you do?

Do you need to get a job? Volunteer? Work out more? Do you have a "bucket list" a mile long, most of it involving things that you and your husband didn't make time to do? If I've learned one thing during this journey, it's that time is not guaranteed. Dale and I talked a lot about what we would do "when we retire." *Never once* did we think that time wouldn't come. So as long as I can afford myself, I'm planning to spend time with my kids, travel, walk on the beach, play golf, and try to figure out the perplexing game of bridge. I will still volunteer at church, and I may have another book or two in my head. If I need to get a job, I'll find one.

If you are still working or currently looking for a job, I encourage you to embrace your situation. It may be a wonderful time to reevaluate your life goals. Do you need to go back to school? Change careers? Apply for a promotion? I taught resume writing and interviewing skills for more than ten years, and I've met with hundreds of people who want to know how to approach the job market. Many of them felt overwhelmed—especially if a career change was imposed by their company or by life.

Many people I've met feel "trapped" by their current circumstances and don't know where to start. If so, treat yourself to a mini makeover. Ask someone whose style you admire to help you "shop your closet." I can't tell you how many vibrant people in their fifties feel like they've "aged out" of the system. They hate—rightly so—the impersonal electronic job-search process that has evolved since they last looked for a job. It's like "dating" to find a new company.

Your attitude plays a huge part in how successful you will be. It's okay to have all of these emotions, but it's not okay to give up. It's time to get your head in the game and to think of this as your "job" for now. There are hundreds of resources available. Go look. You don't even have to leave home to research the best companies to work for in your area, to set up your social media profile, to find networking groups, to apply for open positions, and to polish your resume.

Then you need to tell everyone you know that you're looking for a job—your friends, your hairdresser, and your dentist. If you're conducting a confidential job search, this can be a little tricky. But if people don't know you're looking, how can they help you? Create business cards with a mini resume on the back. Carry them with you. Hand them out.

LinkedIn is the secret weapon in the job-search world. If

you don't have a profile, create one. If you don't know how, get a teenager to help you. Join some groups. Participate in discussions. When you're ready, post your resume. Many job openings that are never advertised to the public are posted only on LinkedIn.

Secret weapon number two is to follow up. I can't tell you how many people I've talked to who submit hundreds of resumes but never hear back from potential employers. I always ask, "How many have *you* contacted?" The answer is always the same: "I don't know how to reach them. I had to submit my resume online, and I don't know who to contact." Too true. But if you really wanted to track down someone, could you make it happen? Probably. Figure it out. Don't give up.

Secret weapon number three is thank-you notes. No one writes them anymore. People fire off a thank-you text and call it good. Think about when you open your own mail. Do you open the fliers and the catalogs first? Nope. You go straight to the hand-addressed notes. Employers are the same. If you send a thank-you-for-the-interview note, they're forced to open it and to pull your folder to the top of the stack. You're probably the only person they interviewed who sent a note. They have to see you in a different light.

So what if you don't need a job? Your kids are grown. You don't have hobbies. You haven't volunteered, and you don't know where to start. What a great problem to have! Now is the time to play "What do I want to be when I grow up?"

Do you have a passion? Did you like to do something when you were younger that you haven't done in years? Do your friends ask you to play golf or bridge—the two most complicated, confusing, confounding games of all time? Now is the time to learn. Trust me—you'll never figure it out, but you'll have a blast trying!

When I moved to Dana Point, I didn't know a single person. I had a housewarming party five months after my move and knew about fifty people to invite—complete with home and e-mail addresses—and most of them came! That didn't happen because I sat at home and waited for people to come knock on my door. You may need to venture outside to see what's available to you, and you may be shocked to learn everything that is going on in your community.

Art and music festivals, classes at the community center, speakers and programs at the library, theater at your local high school, political campaigns, and volunteer opportunities galore! Go to the YMCA, your local hospital, your church, an animal shelter, or a senior center and ask how you might serve there. Ask what services are available for you. The wonderful *Orange County Register*, my local newspaper, publishes a list of volunteer opportunities about once a month. Your paper might too.

Take a class. My local community center is amazing! They offer classes on photography, computers, film, cooking, yoga, martial arts, painting, dancing, foreign languages, bridge, chess— you name it!

Join a Bible study at your church or start one in your home. Join a gym—many have free trial periods and offer membership specials. Find a part-time job. Go through your closets and your garage—what needs to find a new home? After you finish with your stuff, go help a friend.

If nothing else, walk down your block and meet your neighbors. Maybe they need someone to drive them to doctor's appointments or to church, someone to help with yard work, someone to talk to. Organize a block party, ask a neighbor to tea, start a neighborhood watch or dinner club, plant flowers in your yard.

Venture out. Embrace life. Finish well.

Your Story

What is your number one priority in reclaiming your life?

List the steps you're taking to achieve this goal.

If you could choose five activities to do for fun, what would they be?

What opportunities does your community offer for new activities?

Where would you choose to volunteer your time?

Who or what is preventing you from moving toward a rewarding future?

14

Life Is Short—
Get Back in the Game

I've spent a lot of time "in my head" writing this book. It's been an incredibly rewarding and challenging opportunity to meet others who have traveled this road. Through it all I've had the chance to find out where I am with Dale's death, to evaluate who I am, and to embrace what God might have in store for me next. I have met some kindred souls, have grown closer to my children, and—I think—have become a better version of me. Thank you so much for sharing a little of this journey!

I attend two fabulous new Bible study groups who have adopted me and make me feel as though I've always been one of them. My new church, Capo Beach, hasn't replaced Mountain Park—a singular experience I will treasure all my days—but it offers me solace and a place to meet God where I am today. I've made quite a few new friends (including Diana, my "woo-hoo" real estate agent); I'm taking classes in painting and bridge (things I've always wanted to learn but never made time for); and I get to spend a lot of time with my wonderful son, Beau. My daughter, Erin, remains in Amsterdam, but our relationship is loving and strong and she knows she always has a home in Dana Point.

I have a new appreciation for how precious life is, how time can fly by without my ever taking notice, how important it is to tell the people in your life how very valuable they are and, for me, to thank God every day I'm blessed with this life.

Over the past three years, I've tried to take charge of the things I can—my finances, my health, my home, my time. And I've tried to make peace with the things over which I have no control—Dale's death primary among them.

There are many days when I'm still not "successful." I've done my share of "wallowing in it": spending the entire day in my pajamas, thinking I wasn't very good at widowhood, wishing *and* hoping life had taken a different path. But, more days than not, I'm content.

We haven't really talked about being content versus being happy. Do you think there's a difference? If you look up the dictionary definitions, you'll find they each mention the other. But happiness can be a fleeting emotion while contentment is more a state of being. There are some days I have unhappy moments, but I remain content. I remain calm.

When I look back to that sad day when Dale suffered his aneurysm, I'm still amazed at how calm I was. I hope you've had those moments of extreme calm too. At that time, I thought maybe it was the "calm before the storm," but I do believe it was and remains the "peace of God, which transcends all understanding" (Philippians 4:7). So what is that exactly? Like many gifts from God—grace, salvation, the love of Christ—His peace is so powerful that even devout Christians may never fully understand it. To put it into words is nearly impossible.

I went back to the wisdom of the Internet and found a decent answer—in words—at www.gotquestions.org. (Truly, you have to love that!)

The believer who places his or her full confidence in a loving God and is thankful in every circumstance will possess a supernatural peace. An inner calm will dominate the heart. The faithful believer will know peace—his heart and mind are "guarded" by it—despite the tempest raging without. No one, especially those outside of Christ, will be able to fathom that peace. To most, it will remain a mystery how someone can be so serene in the midst of turmoil.

The peace that comes from being in a right relationship with God is not the peace of this world. The world's peace depends on having favorable circumstances: if things are going well, then we feel peaceful; when things go awry, the peace quickly dissipates.[1]

I'm so grateful for this peace from God, and I hope there are days when you feel it too. We didn't do anything to earn it, but—whether we *know* it or not, and whether we *believe* it or not—God has walked with us throughout our lives, and He's *truly* with us right now.

People say, "Oh, how tragic that your husband died. How can you be grateful?" It's a funny thing to put into words, because being grateful in my current circumstance may make it appear I don't *care* that Dale died—which couldn't be further from the truth. But I *am* grateful for my family, my friends, my health, the opportunity to serve, and the chance to embrace my circumstances, to let others see how God is working in my life, and to continue to ponder the great mysteries of faith.

Friedrich Nietzche reminds us: "That which does not kill us makes us stronger." I've read lots of hilarious responses to that philosophy online, but I do agree that the wife who walked into that hospital three years ago is not the same woman who is writing this book. And while I would love to have had the opportunity to live with my husband until we were both older and grayer, I'll take this new version of me.

Earlier I mentioned that we'd address being endlessly busy to fill up our days, minds, and hearts. You may be able to tell I'm a "doer." I'm busy nearly all the time, and my family and friends often give me grief for it. I'll admit that keeping busy keeps my mind occupied on the days when I struggle with life, with solitude, with sorrow.

A friend at Bible study recently told a story about missionaries traveling in Africa with local porters who carried their gear. After a particularly long day of travel, the porters told the missionaries they couldn't travel the next day. When asked why, the porters said they had traveled so far today that they needed to wait until their souls caught up with them. How ironic that the *porters* had to impress upon the *missionaries* the importance of resting in life's busy seasons! It was a "light bulb moment" for me. I'm sure I've traveled far ahead of my soul on many occasions. Sound familiar to you? My new goal is to be aware when my soul is lagging behind and to rest until she can catch up.

Pastor Allan recently gave a great sermon about filling the empty space within. He took a sabbatical to "recharge his batteries" because he'd been running on empty for a couple of years. He and his family went on a long road trip, and then he and his wife went to a retreat specifically designed for pastors and their spouses. He was counting on the retreat to "fix" him and was worried what would happen if it didn't. As fate would have it, the retreat was "terrible, terrible, terrible"—his words, not mine. When he realized the retreat wasn't going to do the trick, he wanted to leave. His darling wife wouldn't let him because *she* would be embarrassed. Forced to occupy his mind while enduring the retreat, he searched through the library available but found nothing to soothe his soul.

Ultimately, he woke up in the middle of the night to the realization that there is no retreat, no friend, no book, and no magic pill that could cure him. The only answer is to spend time with God—deep, life-changing, meaningful, intimate, quality time with the Creator of the universe. (And dropping into church at Christmas and Easter just isn't going to cut it.) For those of us who don't do it often or *ever*, we might ask, "How do I do that?" It may be through prayer, Bible study, meditation, Christ-centered yoga, hiking, or reading Scripture. Literally, it may be as simple as getting on your knees and calling out His name.

Spending time with God not only allows you to look back to the time of your spouse's death in a new light but also enables you to look forward to what life might hold. The vital reality is you are a part of the story of God whether *you* acknowledge *Him* or not. If you haven't had a relationship with Him before, it may take some time for you to build a trusting relationship. If you've had a troubled past with church or if you've been angry with God, it may take even more time and patience. But rest assured the Creator of the universe calls your name, and He is waiting for you to call His.

Building trust with God is like creating a trusting relationship within a friendship or marriage. If you leave at the first sign of trouble, you'll never have a serious, committed association with Him or with anyone else. New relationships are fun and relatively "pain-free" because you have no shared history and you're not really risking anything. The beauty of staying in a committed friendship or marriage is that trust, friendship, love, and devotion are built over time, and they're worth working on. Start by trusting God with something small each week. Even if you're jumping in while angry, disappointed, and confused, by all means take the leap! God can handle it, and He's waiting for you.

So as we near the end of our journey together, have we learned anything?

Losing a loved one brings a fresh awareness of how fragile life can be—a precious gift to be cherished every single day regardless of circumstances. Choose to be present for your life. Do it to honor your spouse. Do it for your children. Do it for *you*. We are the ones who hold ourselves back, and we alone can get back in the game. Life does—indeed—go on. Get dressed and join the living. Don't sweat the small stuff. At the end of your days, not only will it not matter, you won't even remember.

Resolve to do some good. Maybe it just takes getting outside of yourself for a day. Volunteer at your local animal shelter or hospital. Sign up for the weekend mission trip at church. Read to a neighbor or run errands for someone. You won't have to look very far to find someone whose circumstances make your troubles look smaller.

Choose joy. Life is all about choices—where you go to college, the person you marry, which job you accept, where you live, what joy you might find today. This is perhaps the most important choice of all. All of the people you know and love will be happier for it. So will you.

Finally, finish well. None of us knows the time that we have on this earth and—truthfully—we can only imagine what happens after that. But make the most of the time you're given.

> I'm not saying that I have this all together, that I have it made. But I am well on my way, reaching out for Christ, who has so wondrously reached out for me. Friends, don't get me wrong: By no means do I count myself an expert in all of this, but I've got my eye on the goal, where God is beckoning us onward—to Jesus. I'm off and running and I'm not turning back. (Philippians 3:12–14 MSG)

Learning to embrace a life different from the one you imagined isn't something you're going to master by the end of year one, when your family and friends think you should, or when you hope you might. Learn to be happy alone without being desperately lonely. Find a place to store your memories and make peace with them. Realize that you can deeply embrace and honor your marriage to your late spouse and still find contentment, happiness, and maybe even love in the days ahead. Look toward what God has in store for you.

And—every once in a while—spend the day in your pajamas and eat popcorn for dinner. It's okay.

 *Your Future*

What one thing would you like to take charge of right now?

Write down a plan of action to get there.

Describe the most "self-indulgent" thing you've done since your spouse died.

If you could plan something to look forward to, what would it be?

What things do you need to do to make that happen?

Which friends and family would you like to see? Call to make plans.

What does your faith walk look like now? How did you get there?

If you could do one thing to get reconnected with God, what would it be?

"For I know the plans I have for you," declares
the Lord, "plans to prosper you and not to harm you,
plans to give you hope and a future."
(Jeremiah 29:11)

Notes

Chapter Three

1   "These Are the Statistics," Widow's Hope, http://www.widowshope.org/
    first-steps/these-are-the-statistics/.
2   Ibid.

Chapter Four

1   "These Are the Statistics," Widow's Hope.

Chapter Five

1   Lori Tobias, "Family Secrets: Is There a Skeleton in Your Closet?"
    NextAvenue.org, April 24, 2013, http://www.nextavenue.org/family
    -secrets-there-skeleton-your-closet.
2   Ibid.
3   "How to Deal with Bad News," WikiHow.com, http://www.wikihow.com/
    Deal-With-Bad-News.

Chapter Six

1   "Suicide Survivors Face Grief, Questions, Challenges," Harvard Women's
    Health Watch, August 12, 2014, www.health.harvard.edu/blog
    /suicide-survivors-face-grief-questions-challenges-201408127342.
2   Mary Fairchild, "The Bible and Suicide," About.com, http://christianity
    .about.com/od/whatdoesthebiblesay/a/Bible-Suicide.htm.
3   Beth Moore, *Children of the Day* (Nashville: Lifeway Press, 2014), 121.

Chapter Seven

1   Fairchild, "The Bible and Suicide."
2   Josh McDowell, *More Than a Carpenter* (Wheaton, IL: Tyndale House
    Publishers, 1977), 61.

Chapter Eight

1   William Bridges, *Transitions: Making Sense of Life's Changes* (Cambridge, MA: DaCapo Press, 2004), 4.

2   Ibid., 10.

Chapter Eleven

1   Buddy Thomas, "The Widow's Bridge," Superior Planning, http://widows bridge.com/stats.asp.

2   Ibid.

3   Ibid.

4   D. S. Schneider et al., "Dating and Remarriage over the First Two Years of Widowhood," *Annals of Clinical Psychiatry* 8, no. 2 (1996): 51-57, http://www.ncbi.nlm.nih.gov/pubmed/8807029.

5   Janet Kidd Stewart, "Financial Risks Higher for Older Newlyweds," *Chicago Tribune*, June 17, 2007.

6   Brenda Della Casa, "If He Does These 25 Things, You Need to Drop Him Like a Bad Habit," Yahoo.com, February 21, 2015, https://www.yahoo .com/style/if-he-does-these-25-things-you-need-to-drop-him -110665271818.html.

Chapter Thirteen

1   "Grieving before a Death: Understanding Anticipatory Grief," *What's Your Grief?* (blog), September 30, 2013, http://www.whatsyourgrief.com/?s =anticipatory+grief.

2   Ilanit Tal Young et al., "Suicide Bereavement and Complicated Grief," *Dialogues in Clinical Neuroscience* 14, no. 2 (2012): 177–186, www.ncbi .nlm.nih.gov/pmc/articles/PMC3384446.

3   Ibid.

4   "How to Tell the Difference between True and False Guilt," *Life Coach on the Go* (blog), http://lifecoachonthego.com/how-to-tell-the-difference -between-true-and-false-guilt/#sthash.

5   Susan Krauss Whitbourne, PhD, "The Definitive Guide to Guilt," *Psychology Today*, August 11, 2012, https://www.psychologytoday.com/blog/ fulfillment-any-age/201208/the-definitive-guide-guilt.

6   "What Is False Guilt, and How Can I Avoid It?" GotQuestions.org, http:// www.gotquestions.org/false-guilt.html.

7   Jess Walter, *Beautiful Ruins* (New York: HarperCollins, 2012), 4.

8   *The American Heritage Dictionary* (New York: Dell, 1983), 418.

Chapter Fourteen

1   "What Is the Peace That Passes All Understanding?" GotQuestions.org, http://www.gotquestions.org/peace-that-passes-all-understanding.html.

Acknowledgments

Vicki, thank you more than words can say for recommending me to BroadStreet for this project. You are a force of nature, and it's been an amazing blessing to work with you.

Many thanks to David and Carlton at BroadStreet for giving me the opportunity to write this book and for taking a chance on an unknown writer. It was an awesome experience and my privilege to learn from both of you.

Sincerest gratitude to my first readers: Vicki, Rita, Lori, and Lynn. Your notes and fearless edits made this book vastly better than it might have been.

To those of you who shared your stories, ideas, and knowledge for this book, you have my heartfelt thanks, respect, and admiration. You inspired me with your faith, wisdom, honesty, and perseverance.

To my children, Erin and Beau, who served as readers, contributors, and advisors: I'm richly blessed to be your mother, and Dale was so proud to be your dad. I love you more than words can express.

With deepest love and admiration to my mother, Jo: You're an amazing, inspiring woman and an even better mother. I'm sorry we traveled this road, but I know you *know*, and I'm beyond grateful for your love and encouragement.

And, finally, with abiding love and respect to Dale, an incredible husband who was—truly—the most interesting man in the world. Thanks for the memories, Big Daddy.

About the Author

Widow's Might is Kim Knight's first book. Kim holds a master of education in office administration/business education and taught business skills at the college level for many years. During her teaching career, the Colorado Private School Association, KMGH-TV, and *The Denver Post* named her the Colorado Business Skills Teacher of the Year. Kim provides resume writing and interviewing skills guidance as an ongoing ministry, leads Bible study, and has served as a speaker for Christian seminars and retreats. She loves living near here son Beau in Dana Point, California, where she spends way too much time trying to master golf and bridge.